The power of imagination makes us infinite.
~ John Muir ~

Believe you can, and you're halfway there.
~ Theodore Roosevelt ~

A #2 pencil and a dream can take you anywhere.
~ Joyce Meyer ~

Notes

Inspiration 4 Writers

By
M.A. Lee,
Remi Black,
& Edie Roones

Writers Ink Books

Just Start Writing, Write a Book in a Month, and Enter the Writing Business

Inspiration 4 Writers ~ Books 1, 2, and 3

Copyright © 2020 Emily R. Dunn

doing business as Writers' Ink, M.A. Lee, Remi Black, and Edie Roones

First electronic publishing rights: February 2020

All rights are reserved.

No part of this book may be used or reproduced in any manner whatsoever without written permission, except in the case of brief quotations embodied in critical articles and reviews. The unauthorized reproduction or distribution of this copyrighted work is illegal. No part of this book may be scanned, uploaded, or distributed via the Internet or any other means, electronic or print, without the permission of the author or of Writers' Ink.

NOTE FROM THE AUTHOR

This book is a work of non-fiction. Any names, characters, places, and incidents of fiction and nonfiction are cited by the author merely as explanation. Any persons or entity, existing or dead, are also cited by the author for the purposes of explanation. The author does not have any control over and does not assume any responsibility for third-party websites or their content.

Published in the United States of America.

www.writersinkbooks.com

winkbooks@aol.com

Cover Design by Deranged Doctor Design

Table of Contents

Inspiration 4 Writers 3
   M.A. Lee, ... 3
   Table of Contents 5

Just Start Writing 8
   Introduction 8
   Be a Writer ~ 13 Steps for Dancing 10
   Into the Labyrinth ~ A Writing Story 19
   Into Wonderland 24
   Where Do Writers Get Story Ideas? 27
   Building a Book 30
      Index 47

Write A Book in a Month 49
   Introduction 49
      Lessons List 122

Enter the Writing Business 124
   Introduction 124
   Index 210
   Thank you! 214
   Hearts in Hazard by M.A. Lee 215
   Into Death Series by M.A. Lee 215
   Nonfiction by M.A. Lee 216
   Remi Black, fantasy 217
   Edie Roones, fantasy 218

NOTES

Just Start Writing

Inspiration 4 Writers ~ 1

by M.A. Lee

Introduction

Welcome to *Just Start Writing!*

Since you've picked up this little book, you must be curious about writing, for yourself or someone else.

Are stories swirling around? Are ideas to share whirling in your mind? Are you on a carousel, all colors and mirrors with unicorns and griffins and dragons to ride?

That carousel of ideas tempts you to step on and enjoy the ride—yet you hesitate to pass the gate and climb up and select a ride. It's too wondrous, too dreamlike for any reality.

I'm here to tell you to buy the ticket, walk through the gate, spy out the animal you want to ride, and climb on. The carousel is real, not a wonderful dream.

"Wait," you may say. "I've tried before. I've read writing guidebooks until my eyes glaze over. I joined a writing group. I scan Pinterest and read the links. Writing just—it looks overwhelming. It can't be that easy."

Writing *is* that easy.

You want this dream, don't you? Hasn't the dream of writing persisted? Don't you keep jotting ideas down? Aren't you investigating and exploring because you can't release the dream?

I know. That was me, too. I've wanted to be a published writer since the Dark Ages[1]. For years I tinkered with stories, yet I never pursued my dream. I played with the idea of climbing aboard the carousel.

A few years ago I decided to get serious about my dream. I set a deadline to publish my first book in 2015—and I succeeded! Since then, I haven't looked back. As M.A. Lee and my other two pseudonyms, I've published 30 titles, mostly fiction. This little guidebook is part of a collection of nine titles specifically for new writers.

Now people ask, *"How did you start writing?"* and *"How do you come up with all of those stories?"*

Writers ask, *"How do I start writing?* and *"Where do you get your ideas?"*

See the difference in those questions? Most people don't care about the process. Writers want the process so they can apply it to their own carousels of struggles.

That's our first admission, you and me: Writing is a struggle.

- Time to Write
- What to Write
- Creating sense out of jumbled fragments.
- Discovering characters and plot.
- Playing with words so they say what we mean.

If these questions are yours—*How do I start writing?* and *Where do you get your ideas?*—then this little book is for you.

Read on. Glean what you need. Climb on that carousel—and *Just Start Writing*!

---

[1] Seriously, around 5th grade, I started my dream of writing books. I had realized—finally—that a person wrote the *great book* that I had just finished. Someone wrote *it*, and I could write books, too!

BE A WRITER ~ 13 STEPS FOR DANCING

How do I start writing?

That's the question that a former student recently asked. He knew I had launched my writing business—gone pro, you know.

I spent my teaching years telling my students much more information than they ever wanted to know for our daily lessons. I did the same thing with him. Couldn't help myself. 13 Steps, in no particular order.

My former student contacted me about his great book idea. He wanted guidance on how to start writing. I texted back—several long texts. I've now expanded my answers to him for you all.

Here we go.

STEP 1] JUST START WRITING

Who do you want to write about?

What story do you want to tell?

Just launch into an event with that character. You don't have to start at the beginning or the end. Whatever is swirling, get it down.

Once that scene is out, give a little thought to that character.

People connect to characters they like. Develop a like-able protagonist (you know, a real person with honor and humility, dreams and goals, a bit of crazy wildness, and a whole raft of kindness). Don't forget to give that protagonist angst that can be overcome.

Here's a blatant self-promotion: I could have advised my student to purchase *Discovering Your Novel*. For total newbies and people stuck in their manuscripts, *DiscNovel* has all sorts of guides from idea to finished manuscript. It's designed to help a writer complete a book in one year. Week to week guidance, with charts! A one-stop reference on world building, basic character development and plot structure, revision, and proofreading. Beginner writers don't really need anything else....

- If the problem's not the words but the writer, then change your mindset. When this is the case, you need *Think like a Pro,* seven lessons that will help you change your mindset and move you from dabbler to—well, thinking like a professional writer.

STEP 2] BE CERTAIN OF YOUR PEEPS

The protagonist's allies need to be like-able, too. Especially since we might *kill* a couple of them off during the course of the book.

Kill them? Yes, we can kill people off.

You don't have to do that, of course. You can do whatever you want with your characters and stories. You can do anything!

Isn't that freeing? You are in charge of your own writing.

You can break the rules and follow them.

You can ignore people's advice and criticisms and critiques.

Or revise based on that advice and criticisms and critiques.

It's your writing. You're in charge. I want to say that over and over. No one else can write the book in your head. You do it. Start at the end. In the middle. Second chapter on. Anywhere you want.

Kill people off. Birth new ones.

The *ONLY* thing that matters is that your writing gradually forms a coherent story.

Oops. "How do I do that?" you ask.

Next dance step, please.

STEP 3] USE PATTERNS AND MODELS

And when you use those patterns and models, start adjusting them to your story to create a unique twist.

The foundations of character building and plot structure are the same and have been the same for thousands upon thousands of years. Every decade or so new terminology comes out, but the essence remains constant.

Patterns and models are called archetypes. These are worldwide patterns—which means your audience for this story will be worldwide.

For plot, use the Archetypal Story Pattern.

- ASP creates a roller-coaster plot flow with suspense and tension built in.
- Check out Christopher Vogler's *Writers' Journey*, easily researched on the internet. That's an excellent resource for any beginning writer.
- Most of the new *stuff* about writing that has come out since Vogler's seminal book just builds on Vogler's source—Joseph Campbell, who built on Carl Jung. You can't go wrong with Jung.
    - It's like the Master Teacher stuff, four versions that I endured during three decades of teaching. The same information was re-packaged to look new and shiny with lots of new jargon to make you think you're getting new until you look closely and see all the similarities with a few minuscule differences. When I think of all those hours in meetings about the re-packaged new-old that was pushed! Let's just say I could have taken several long vacations every five years or so.

Most writers talk about Beats, which is built on Freytag's Pyramid: that artificial constraint on story. Others talk about using tropes; without a strong theme the tropes create a mishmash of scenes.

For characters, I could have advised my former student to check out my recent *Discovering Characters*, a one-stop manual that covers the different archetypal characters and other classifications, relationships as well as allies and enemies, and progressions, transgressions, and transitions.

From individual archetypes to team roles, from character angst to the couple bond, this book helps all writers learn (and remember) ways to turn the simple image of character into a fully fleshed person with skeleton and flesh and organs, especially the heart.

BTW, those previous two paragraphs list things to consider for your primary, secondary, and tertiary characters, even if you decide to ignore my #BSP.

Whatever you use to develop characters and plot, write your basic story. When that rough draft is complete, then consider tropes and check that your story is following the Beats. You'll discover that the archetypes not only kept your story on-track but also moving from beginning to end, even through the dreaded middle.

STEP 4] BE A PRO WITH THE MANUSCRIPT

Before you get too far into the rough draft, set up your manuscript properly. It's easier to do at the beginning than waiting at the end.

Format the manuscript just like you did for essays in college and high-school.

That means 1-inch margins, double-spaced, and with no additional space between paragraphs ~ unless it's nonfiction, like this little guidebook.

Use automatic wrap, which means that you let the words flow from one line to the next without your interference. You only hit "enter" when you need to start the next paragraph.

Set paragraph tabs at .25.

Center your title and all headings.

A handy little organizer for your MS is STYLES on the HOME ribbon.

- Pick normal for body text, Heading 1 for Book Title, Heading 2 for Chapter Titles. Hover your mouse over the style type and right-click to select modify. You can change fonts and paragraph elements (such as removing the "Widow/Orphan" control.
- When you finish the manuscript, Styles will assist you in creating a table of contents. Under REFERENCE is the "Table of Contents", an automatic generator.

Use page numbers for drafts. This will help you as you proof. When you reach your final copy, follow submission guidelines.

- If you are submitting to traditional publishers, find out the publisher's submission guidelines and follow them. Styles will ease any changes.
- For self-publication, use the submission guideline templates available from your online distributor. For example, e-books at Amazon don't need page numbers; paperbacks do.

STEP 5] BE WILLING TO LOSE CONTROL

If the characters grab the story and you feel like you're just along for the *write*, celebrate! That's inspired writing. The angels have graced those words.

Writing can seem like a real slog. Then we have those moments—minutes, hours—when the story takes hold, the words just fly. When we finish the session, we look back and realize we may need to flesh things out a bit, yet the ideas that appeared from nowhere are great.

These inspired moments are gifts of the creative muse. Celebrate them.

Never hesitate to change anything planned. The creative muse loves anything planned because she loves twisting ideas around. A plan gives her elements to work with. Create as detailed of a plan as you want then willingly abandon it wherever the muse dances on.

Then return to the plan when the muse releases you.

Always celebrate great writing achievements:

- completing a chapter
- reaching major points of the rough draft
- completing the rough draft
- completing the final draft
- finishing the proof-plus on the book
- getting a great cover
- publishing the dang thing
- discovering the next great story idea
- having the inspired writing moments

These are all extremely important. In writing, the rewards (which are rarely monetary) come few and far between.

STEP 6] BE TWISTY WITH PLOT

You can't have a wonderful protagonist unless you have a twisty wicked antagonist.

When my former student asked for advice on how to write his first novel, he shared the cranial bone of his idea which gave a strong hint about his central antagonist. I'll share the bit of bone here, since many stories, including the recent Hunger Games series and the 1970's *Logan's Run,* are built on the same brain bone.

BTW, that's the reason ideas cannot be copyrighted, only the form that your idea takes through the words you put on the page. When some steals your words, word after word after word, page by page, scene by scene, then that's breaking copyright . . . and you can go get them!

So, in the bits of advice *for him* that I'm sharing *with you*, the conflict came next.

I told him that his antagonist sounded like an institution running a supposedly Utopian society, which means he had a masked dystopia. That's always fun to write with the protagonist's slowly dawning realization followed by an attempt to convince allies of the dystopia and rally them and others to fight!

Logan's Run does the masked dystopia pattern exceptionally well. As flawed as the film of the novel is, it still does an excellent job of shocking the audience with the switch from Utopia to Dystopia.

- Along with the protagonist, the reader has a double-surprise following that realization followed by a second double-surprise with the protagonist's allies. Surprising the reader is important in

any story.
- Then comes the quadruple-obstacle of escaping the dystopia—problem, problem, problem, problem—and still the writer is not finished with surprises. Escape only starts up a whole new set of shocks.
- If you want to understand surprising the audience, you can study *Logan's Run*.
    - It is highly dated and chauvinistic, which makes it offensive to modern sensibilities.
    - If you want to see how much society has changed in less than 50 years, the film is the exemplar as a product of its time and the patriarchal mindset, to be much derided now. Throw popcorn at the viewing screen.
    - However, it's also a well-written story with constant movement that gets the necessary surprises right.

Be careful as you consider *any* advice about antagonists, mine or other people's. The advice may seem simplistic; it never is. Many great writers have whole novels fall apart when they haven't created strong antagonists. The weaker the antagonist, the weaker your protagonist.

STEP 7] BE WILLING TO HAVE MINOR ANTAGONISTS

Besides this major antagonist, you will need minor antagonists more "local" than the mastermind. Make each antagonist more difficult to defeat as the story progresses.

Minor antagonists can be minions of the major antagonist or can work independently. An independent bad guy is certainly an unexpected twist.

Minions take various forms:

- Most are simply pawns, following orders without considering consequences.
- Some are scary evil, working for the antagonist because they enjoy evil.
- A few are reluctant, compelled by circumstance or coerced by the major antagonist to maintain that alliance.
    - These characters offer great opportunities for angst.
- The best minions have plans to step in when the major antagonist falls. When we have this minion, we have the chance to kill off the major antagonist at the 75% mark of the book only to have the replacement step up and be more evil.

STEP 8] BE GLOBAL WITH AN ANTAGONIST

Having an institution as an antagonist will strengthen the protagonist.

Defeating the institution will seem impossible. Defeating each minion should give a key to unlock the walls guarding the institution.

The institution might be short-term planning and merely needs persuasion to be overcome. Or its long-term planning needs a take-down.

The protagonist can enlist a counter-institution or release devastating information. The institution may not be defeated and destroyed completely. It could be blocked, caged, or weakened.

And the institution may become the major antagonist for the whole series of books you decide to write.

Step 9] Be Angsty

Strong protagonists, twisty antagonists, and clever surprises drive great story-telling. These three give all writers angst. When writers do their writing right, they also give their readers angst.

Work in two betrayals. Have one early (before the 20% mark) and the other before the ¾-mark of the story (around 60-75%).

People hate betrayal. They remember it like acid burning their memories and their soul. Some people never quite recover from betrayal. Others keep waiting on the traitors to redeem themselves—that might could happen, mostly doesn't.

The betraying character is often called a Shapeshifter. We have two forms:
- The character who seems to be working for the antagonist but is not. Either this character was trapped into the appearance of alliance with evil or this character is working on redemption.
- The other Shapeshifter is a true traitor, the double agent, the one who appears to support the protagonist but has been working for the antagonist the whole time.
- Save the exposure of the true traitor for the latter part of your novel.

Step 10] Use Surprise

When you're trying to think of how to surprise the reader and your protagonist, you need to reject what most people would think of. Think harder. Not the first or second event you think of; go to the third or fourth.

Surprises keep stories moving and readers reading. When you can tie multiple surprises to your antagonists, you have great story telling.
- Always think outside the box of what normal people would do. People were shocked by *Gone Girl* and *The Sixth Sense*. I figured both out from the promotions, but then I've taught story structure and character development for decades. It's hard to surprise me.
- Tilt your head sideways with your betrayals and antagonists and angst and surprises.

Red Herrings are examples of surprises. These are characters who distract from the major antagonist.

Originally in the mystery genre, a Red Herring is a character who can be equally guilty of the crime. Except for a few planted and well-hidden clues, RHerrings could be the actual murderer.

Step 11] Be Disciplined with Writing

Every writer—fiction / nonfiction, prose / poetry, book / film / playscript—needs discipline to succeed.

Discipline begins with achievable writing goals. Think weekly then divide into daily. Write your planned new words every day—no exceptions except injury or major events (celebrations like family holidays and weddings and graduations and the like).

- When I became serious about publishing, it took me a whole year to change my mindset from hobby writer to pro writer. My journey became the 7 lessons shared in *Think like a Pro*.
- I started with 1,000 words daily as my minimum word count. That's about 2 hours (think two 500-word essays. Practice allows the words to come faster. Since that first true writing year, I've upped my word count, and I celebrate every time I achieve more than my new minimum.

You can break up your writing sessions into smaller increments. Few of us are lucky enough to indulge in long daily writing sessions. Be realistic. Consider your daily obligations. Pick an achievable goal—less than you truly want, such as 500 words.

- 500 words builds to 3,000 a week which is 12,000 a month. In five months of steady writing at this level—500 words per day for six days each week—you achieve a 60,000-word novel, or two novellas or ½ of an epic.

Don't fret when a bad week occurs. Every day is a new day. Every week is a new week.

Creating a devotion to writing is essential. Maintaining that devotion is a constant struggle. The longer you are away, the harder it is to return. Writing every day makes it much easier to recover from the bad days and the bad weeks.

STEP 12] BE A TRACKER

Track what you do in each writing session. Track where you're going for each session.

And don't forget to be willing to go off-track (Step 5).

1st, Track your Word Counts for this week and this month.

Keep a running word count to monitor success. Celebrate every major word count ~ 5,000 > 10,000 > 25,000 > 50,000 > 100,000 for the year and more and more. You can easily achieve these numbers throughout the year.

Maintaining this simple weekly word count will be the *hardest* thing you have done and will ever do. Maintaining it is *CRUCIAL*.

The building word count of the manuscript helps you feel success. Fall off? Hop back on. Any extra words make up for the falling-off days—which will happen.

2nd, Track your Tasks for this week and this month, this season and this year.

Track what occurred in each writing session by outlining it afterwards on a simple legal pad. This has a dual benefit:

- You don't get bored with the story by planning too much beforehand.
- You have a running list of events and basic info about scenes. When you finish, you can store this basic list, updated, with the final manuscript—which is helpful when you need to return to the MS months or years after.

3rd, Track your Projects and the Stages of those Projects.

You have goals that you want to accomplish. Divide those into the projects with tasks that are necessary to accomplish those goals.

Keep up with what you plan to accomplish as well as what you have accomplished.

Know the stages for your projects. Any writing can be divided into Ideas > Rough > Draft > Edit > Publishing. Each of these stages also has its own incremental divisions for completion. Success occurs when you know where you are, where you've been, and where you're going. Nebulous thinking about the projects and stages and incremental divisions fosters an overwhelming dizzy ride. Carousels aren't really dizzy rides when you're on them.

STEP 13] BE A FRIEND TO JOT LISTS

Drum Roll, please. Here's the last step so you can enjoy the writing dance. Of course, with all advice, take it or leave it. What works for some will not work for others.

However ~

End each session and begin each session with a jot-list.

The ending jot-list will list what should occur next. Never write until the words run dry. Write for your allotted time, then make notes about what will happen next.

Begin each session by reviewing the ending jot-list then create a new list before you start writing. Handwriting this list of words and phrases seems to engage the brain more than typing it does.

You may not be able to hit all of the ideas in the next writing session. Those ideas will then head into the next session—or will be held in reserve for the appropriate upcoming scene. Always transfer the ideas over. Never trash them.

- The impish creative muse will not be amused if you trash ideas that she's given you. Don't offend the muse; she's got prickly thorns.
- These ending/beginning lists do not count in your daily words.
- When away from the writing session, going about your daily life, the impish muse will tickle your subconscious brain, and new ideas for your story will continue to develop.

There. That's the 13 steps for anyone wanting to *Just Start Writing*—whether it's a novel or a nonfiction work or poetry or a play. This advice works for any type of writing, including emails at work.

BSP 1 ~ If you truly want to write your first novel—or you want to complete that manuscript that you shoved into a drawer a few years ago because it wasn't working, then *Discovering Your Novel* can help.

#BPS 2 ~ If the problem was characters, then try my *Discovering Characters* and *Discovering Your Plot*.

#BSP 3 ~ If you are struggling with the transition from writing as a hobby to writing seriously so you can become a professional writer, you will find the seven lessons in *Think like a Pro* helpful.

BSP 4 ~ Want something to keep you on-track with projects and word counts? Try the *Think/Pro* planner for writing, with daily word counts and project tracking, monthly & seasonal reviews and previews, and additional tips and guidance to help you with the transition from newbie to Pro.

Think like a Pro and the *Think/Pro* planner are available in print as well as electronic editions; the *Discovering* set is not yet available in paperback. That *will* happen soon, but for now I'm *busy*. As always, all the writing is AFM, all mine.

INTO THE LABYRINTH ~ A WRITING STORY

Into the Labyrinth is Remi Black's story of her passage to publication. She graciously shares it with Just Start Writing since it fits the focus of this book.

I have written stories all my life. With *Dream a Deadly Dream*, I thought, "Here's a story with intriguing characters and a twisty plot and a catchy title. This is *the book*. This is the first book that will be published by the official big publishing houses."

I sent out the original manuscript with great hopes.

Back it bounced, usually with a "nice" rejection letter attached.

- I call those rejections "nice" because the comments would be things like "great writing" or "I loved this story" or "I really liked the characters" or something else that gave me hope.
- Just like a journey into the labyrinth, reaching the end of the ball of string and finding the two-horned monster waiting, when I reached the end of the letter my spirits would be crushed.
- What monster waited for me in that last paragraph? The reason for the rejection. The editors' statements always varied:
    - This book's not magical enough OR it doesn't have enough fighting OR it's not different enough from the other books in our catalog OR it's not like our other books OR it's not romantic enough OR it's too romantic for our readers.

Hopes raised only to be crushed. Replies that confused me when I considered what to do next. I was wondering in the black maze without a light.

After a year of this, I decided to shelve *Dream a Deadly Dream*. "Later," I told it.

1ST BIT OF STRING ~

KEEP WRITING. WRITERS HAVE MORE THAN ONE STORY TO TELL.

While *Dream/Deadly* was bouncing back and forth, I worked on *Sing a Graveyard Song*.

I muddled through that manuscript, a slow go, trying to increase the "fighting" and add more "magical" and reduce the "romance" while keeping enough of it to satisfy me. Then I would jerk out what I added in because it didn't really fit the story. I wrote and revised and trashed and re-wrote and wrote again and again revised.

Early in the writing of *Sing/Grave*, I realized that the story of Alstera (one of the two protagonists in *Dream/Deadly*) would require multiple books.

Alstera started as a side character in *Dream/Deadly*, but here she was in *Sing/Grave* taking charge of the story. She had morphed from the archetypal ally side-character into a full-blown protagonist.

A full-blown protagonist has her own issues and conflicts. And Alstera had a compelling backstory.

Guess what? In thinking about Alstera, the creative muse offered up another story with her character. Great Scot! I was writing a series!

2ND BIT OF STRING

A SINGLE CHARACTER CAN GIVE SEVERAL NOVELS.

Which meant that I would have to back up to write the opening story.

An unexpected monster, but I knew I could handle the novel. I had completed *Dream/Deadly*. I would complete *Sing/Grave*, no matter what. A third novel was nothing, especially when the fourth was intriguing me, drawing me on.

3RD BIT OF STRING

PAY ATTENTION TO WHAT THE CHARACTER AND STORY NEED.

Somewhere around the midpoint of *Sing/Grave*, I ran across Robert Heinlein's 5 Rules of Writing.

1. *You must write*. Okay, I had that one down.
2. *You must finish what you write*. Well, I still had a lot of stories only started and half-completed manuscripts, but I was beginning to finish more and more manuscripts. *Sing/Grave* was giving me fits, but I was writing it. I could see its end. I had two more stories to tell after that one.
3. *You must refrain from rewriting, except to editorial order*. Ooookay. But the editorial orders (and agents' comments) that I was getting weren't really helping the story. And no contract (a key element that Heinlein required before he embarked on a revision) was in the offing.

A handful of years after my first encounter with the Rules, I began reading pushback about them, especially on Rule 3. The best explanation and confirmation about this rule that I received, years after I reached my own conclusion, came from Dean Wesley Smith, which you can read here
https://www.deanwesleysmith.com/heinleins-rules-chapter-six/ and here
https://www.deanwesleysmith.com/heinleins-rules-chapter-five/

So, continuing Heinlein's Rules~

4. You must put the work on the market. Okay, did that.
5. You must keep the work on the market until it is sold. Okay, but I ran out of market.

With Rule 3, following other people's advice wasn't helping *Sing/Grave*. I needed to finish it. I needed to finish the story that *I* wanted to tell. Once that was done, I could let others read it for plot holes and character discrepancies and the like.

4TH BIT OF STRING

FINISH WHAT YOU START. *WITHOUT* LISTENING TO OTHER PEOPLE'S COMMENTS.

THOSE COMMENTS CAN *KILL* YOUR STORY.

So I followed my bit of string.. I ignored the rejection letter comments and wrote the *Sing/Grave* in my head.

I think quite a number of new writers fall into this mistake of listening to other people's comments about their stories.

- Early on, when I wanted to be in a critique group, I couldn't find one close enough for regular meetings.
- When I actually found an organization within a half-hour of my residence, the mid-week meetings ran late, late, late when my alarm woke me at 5 a.m. Nix that opportunity. Jobs pay bills.
- When I found a critique group that wasn't going to run late, late, late, I thought the people in the group—as unpublished as I was—were a little arrogant when they talked about other writers who were published long-term. They nitpicked little things in a paragraph rather than trying to get an overall snapshot of the story.
- Then it dawned on me that I wanted publication. Here I was, listening to people who weren't published. Bam! Out of this new-found critique group I went. I needed professionals who would give advice about craft and process and the business.

5TH BIT OF STRING

FIRST READERS ONLY READ FINISHED MANUSCRIPTS.

The best First Readers take a hard look at the story, which may require additions and revisions, gutting and enhancing. Listen to the best ones.

So I completed *Sing/Grave* and its revisions and corrections.

Then I turned the manuscript over to my First Readers, people who would critique it, not gush over it or criticize it. I evaluated the MS based on their comments then revised, and edited again.

Finished, I sent it out again, following Heinlein's Rulse 4 and 5. That book began its own journey of back and forth with its own growing collection of confusing rejections.

While *Sing/Grave* journeyed and *Dream/Deadly* haunted me, I launched into *Weave a Wizardry Web*.

Weave/Web became a massive undertaking. It drove me crazy for a long, long time. Launching into that backstory didn't flow as easily as I anticipated.

Early in the draft, another character demanded that her story control *Weave/Web*. Alstera, for whom I wrote this book was being written, had to take a strong sub-primary role.

I wrote sketch after sketch. Some scenes had six different versions. Yet this demanding book still refused to come together.

6TH BIT OF STRING

NO MATTER HOW HARD THE BOOK IS, NEVER THROW ANYTHING AWAY.

You may need to take a step-away from the book in order to get a handle on it. In the time while you're gone, pursuing other writing projects until you can devote more time to this monster, the creative muse will dance around with the story.

My step-away from *Weave/Web* wasn't my decision. That was Divine God making me step-away so I could see what needed to be done. I wouldn't have stepped back on my own.

Life presented a true minotaur for me to battle. It frightened me and broke my heart and re-built my view of self and required sacrifices I had never intended to make. When I started fighting that beast, I stopped writing altogether.

Then, deep in the battle, out of the darkness erupted a story I hadn't expected. It burst forth, nearly full blow. Not fantasy but romantic suspense: *Quelle surprise*! In one-hour increments I took respite from battling that true minotaur. Gradually, over two years, the new story worked toward completion. Once done, I started a second romantic suspense. Those novels helped me survive the labyrinth and its resident minotaur.

Once the battle ended, though, I didn't grab hold of the Alstera series. Somehow, during those of the dark passages, I lost the writing goal. Instead of picking up my writing and going full tilt at hopeless windmills, I just tinkered with writing and poured my creative energies into my day job.

Here's what I think.

I tinkered because the greatest monster in the labyrinth—traditional publishing—barred the gate to the treasure I wanted.

My simple dream, publication of my writing—not riches, not fame, just people reading my stories and wanting more of them—that dream would never be fulfilled. I couldn't write the stories in my brain if I followed what some distant editor was demanding: more cyberpunk, more vampires, more sensuality, more curse words for a hard edge, more this, more that.

What was the point of starting another blind battle against the monstrous gate-keepers in the glass towers?

7th Bit of String

Pay attention to the world around you.

Changes happen without your noticing.

The change that happened for me? The one that helped me defeat the minotaur of traditional publishing that once trapped my writing in a black maze? Amazon's Kindle.

The Kindle Reader revolutionized publishing. Individuals—*indies* could now self-publish and sell their works. The early writers who did so discovered a public hungry for books that the glass-tower traditional publishers weren't buying.

I jumped on board the Kindle revolution late. When I started, I focused first on the novels that God gave me to survive that obligation. I needed a third book to launch with those two. I gave myself three years to publish those—and I made my deadline.

Then came the turn of my Enclave series: *Dream/Deadly*, which still haunted me, and *Sing/Grave*, both ready and waiting. Yet before I published either book, I had to finish *Weave/Web*.

Weave/Web was its own black labyrinth, a deep cavern of winding passages and re-doubling dilemmas and backtracking abysses. More than determination was necessary to make sense of the chaos of all those rewritten sketches. Patience. Clear thinking. No other work lurking in wait. Nothing unexpected ready to pounce. Persistence. Resolve. Creativity. I needed all of those.

8ᵀᴴ Bit of String

Never be daunted.

Tackle large projects a step at a time.

I organized everything. And launched the writing in late May. It was a mess. It wouldn't come together. The writing just wasn't going the way that it needed to.

I defeated a good portion of the problem when another character chimed in, demanding his own part of the story. I had to backtrack over a hundred pages to add him to scenes and develop him properly. Still, the story began to advance.

9ᵀᴴ Bit of String

A story will tell you what it needs.

Listen to those small urgings.

The final step that brought everything together, the step that defeated the beast that blocked the book and brought me back into the daylight was a fourth character who came to me in a dream—a nightmare. Once I had his voice, I had the key to the whole maze of *Weave/Web*.

The story began flowing, a river rushing out of the unlit passages, flushing out all of the ideas that had hidden in the darkness, afraid of the monstrous chaos.

Once I finished *Weave/Web,* I returned to the pure joy of *Dream/Deadly*. I updated the novel to match the events that sprang into *Weave/Web*, and then I picked up *Sing/Grave* for its updating.

10ᵀᴴ Bit of String

Don't let the past hang over you.

In the midst of my struggles with Weave/Web, I uprooted myself, left my job, and moved closer to my beloved mountains. As I packed for that major move, I found that ream of rejection letters.

And I shredded them. It was a cleansing experience.

Into Wonderland

Alice followed the White Rabbit into a hole that dropped her into a strange world.

Writing is like that, a hole into a strange wonderland. A project is an intriguing white rabbit luring us to follow even as it reminds us that the project has to meet a deadline or be "late for that important date".

In autumn, with the glorious blaze of the changing leaves, my thoughts always turn to the projects for the next year. Even with projects still for this year, the blazing ideas for the new crowd in, trying to push out the ones that I need to finish.

Before I became disciplined with those projects—a lesson it took over a year to learn (I know; I'm slow)—I would have allowed myself to nibble that sweet biscuit of a novel or drink that tea of a nonfiction book.

I've learned not to graze into upcoming projects unless a sure and specific benefit is offered.

Wonderland operates by its own skewed rules. Writing is the same kind of Wonderland. Unlike the humdrum work world, we can pick the biscuit we want to eat and keep nibbling until the project fills up the house. We can add in our wondrous encounters with the sly Cheshire cat and the strange caterpillar and Tweedle Dee and Tweedle Dum before taking tea with the Mad Hatter and the Dormouse.

As long as we remember the rules by which our skewed Wonderland operates.

Rule 1

For writers, for anyone pursuing the haunting dream, Never stop.

Never stop writing. Get to the end. And continue. Don't leave the Wonderland. Once we visit the Red Queen, we have many more places to explore.

If you are pursuing traditional publishing, write the second and third and fourth books while the first one is submitted to editors and agents.

If you are an indie writer, having come to the Indie World after giving up on the Trads or bypassing the Trads entirely, the greatest reward is having others read your writing and praise it.

Rule 2

Treat your work professionally.

If it's the dream you want, pursue it like a job. Present the best typescript possible for your readers, and hire professionals to polish the manuscript before you publish it.

People who are content editors and proofreaders enable your *words* to look as professional as you need them to be.

Accept that nothing wonderful ever came easily.

You may hear of other writers who game the system. Avoid that. You will be happier if you keep your work honorable. That flamingo may fly off with some else's croquet ball but not yours. You demand that your flamingo play the game correctly.

Many shysters have attached themselves to the world of writing. Disguising themselves as vanity publishers or developmental editors or marketing gurus, they want to separate you from your money. Don't let them.

The writing community can be a warm and welcoming place, like a teapot with a splash of gin for a nice hot toddy. Even in safe havens, evil will lurk. Don't be lured in; don't be a curmudgeon. Use circumspection and wise business practices in dealing with others.

And remember that a contract is a contract.

Rule 3

Humans are visual, and the first attractors to books are the covers.

Cover designers are more essential than editors. Some people will drop $4000.00 on a developmental editor then create their own cover or buy a generic one for $50.00.

What's the old saying? "A man who is his own lawyer has a fool for a client." Well, that works for cover designers as well.

Covers should entice readers into the Wonderland of your work. This is one expense you cannot skimp.

Take the time to search the internet and find a designer whose aesthetic fits the tone of the book that you want.

After an 18-month search, the designers I found are professional and creative and clever, adding details that I would never think of. An excellent cover designer can take a few glimmering words of direction ("this is the fire book") and create an enchanting cover that captures the novel, whether in an abstract way or more realistically.

Cover designs should make your manuscript feel special.

Acknowledgements

Nothing I have accomplished would be possible without my kin and kith.

Thank God they are positive examples of friends and family.

When we do surface from Wonderland, our minds are a little confused by tea parties and our hearts assaulted by the heart-card soldiers. We want to curl up beneath a kindly tree. We can't, though. The real world calls to us, and our kin and kith help us with that transition.

Family and friends bolster and encourage and diss our stories in positive ways. Mine love me and ground me in reality and keep my dreams soaring. They critique rather than criticize and praise when praise is deserved.

And they let me have the time I need for writing and pursuing my dream.

WRITING IS A SOLITARY BUSINESS.

Writers spend their "free" time in their brains, working out characters and plots and considering themes and motifs. The best support system for writers are friends who give strong critiques, who spot problems, and who give their honest opinions of the story.

The best support system that I have ever found are my two First Readers, Diane and Steve. I can never thank them enough for giving me encouragement and criticisms.

Life throws us unexpected roadblocks, high walls that block our view of the future, and twisting passages that can steal our hearts. On our Wonderland journey, we can encounter darkness and monsters and might lose our way. Family and friends keep us progressing.

Without their love and support, we can achieve our dreams.

WHERE DO WRITERS GET STORY IDEAS?

I'm a longtime lover of light romance in a historical time frame.

When I started writing my own stories, it was only natural that several of the novels in my Hearts in Hazard series would have more than a nod to the precursors who formed my love of the genre.

The first Hearts in Hazard, *A Game of Secrets*, is my attempt at a smuggler's story, à la Daphne Du Maurier's *Jamaica Inn*.

The Dangers of Secrets is my homage to Georgette Heyer's *Cousin Kate*.

The Key with Hearts curled around the same concept as Heyer's *A Civil Contract*, a marriage-of-convenience story with only a touch of romance. Mine, however, added inconvenient threats, mistakes and missed opportunities, and attempted murder.

My personal favorite by Heyer is *Venetia*, with *The Unknown Ajax* only a whisker behind. You can't go wrong with either of those books. Both are excellent romances as well as light comedy, and *Ajax* goes one better by adding mystery and suspense to the story. *Venetia*, however, has characters that appeal just a little bit more.

The Key for Spies has more in common with Georgette Heyer's historical novels, where the main focus is on the events rather than the relationships--although the relationships will bring tears to your eyes and we readers have pleasurable meetings with old friends from other Heyer books.

After years of reading and re-reading Heyer's light romances and mysteries, I encountered her *An Infamous Army*, which concludes with her carefully researched depiction of the Battle of Waterloo, when Wellington and his allies finally and completely defeated Napoleon Bonaparte. *AIA* is a precursor for my *K4Spies* although it is not a direct inspiration.

An Infamous Army is not one of Heyer's light-hearted joys. More than anything else, it is an historical novel, and its meticulous detail is off-putting for many. I don't remember my first reading of it. When I finally returned, with another decade of life behind me, I found a much greater understanding of Heyer's story and much greater patience with her development of it.

If you are a history buff, with Napoleon and Wellington in your sights, *AIA* is a wonderful source. The whole back half is a close depiction of the details of this significant battle.

Heyer's work is so well-researched (as many sources on the internet inform us) that the novel was required reading at Sandhurst, a British military college. Heyer was even invited to lecture at Sandhurst. Here is only one source ~ https://thebeaumonde.com/an-infamous-army/. Many other sources abound: search Heyer, the title, and Sandhurst or military college, and the search engine will provide multiple sites for perusal.

The original ideas swirling for my book, *The Key for Spies*, were soldier and Wellington. Those two words started my mind spinning. I *had* to discover the reason a British soldier would become a spy.

Then comes the next question ~ When and where in the Regency era would a soldier *need* to become a spy?

I knew of Wellington's Peninsular campaign (thank you, Ms. Heyer), and so I dug a little bit, looking for soldiers not in battle. Research into reconnaissance planted the story in Spain, and everything else developed from there.

For example, Miriella Teba developed, leader of a guerrilla band, fighting against French soldiers garrisoned in the local town. Her world developed around her. The French officer LeCuyer sprang forth, searching for the guerrillas and any English spies.

Then came Jesus, Angelo, and the other guerrillas. Elixane sprang into the story around chapter 10, necessitating going back and adding her at earlier places.

I have enjoyed my journey with *Key for Spies*. I have researched plants for gardens--jacarandas and cypress walks. I've explored new house plans and new recipes. The dinner party Miri unwillingly hosts for the French officers is a dinner based on authentic Spanish recipes that I would love to try. I have also become enamored of the afternoon *siesta* and wistful about breakfast on the terrace, with lots and lots of coffee.

ALL OF THIS FORMS THE ANSWER TO THE ORIGINAL QUESTION:

WHERE DO WRITERS GET STORY IDEAS?

Whether we realize it or not, all our previous story experiences—reading books and watching films—guide our writing choices. We take elements of events and characters from everywhere; we can't help it.

Those elements then spin into story ideas.

Before we know it, we've spun a scenario into scenes and chapters.

My smuggler story is nothing like *Jamaica Inn*. My marriage-of-convenience is nothing like *A Civil Contract*.

We writers don't track the stories of others when we write our own books. Our stories evolve from their own characters and situations and conflict.

That leads to the next place that gives ideas for stories.

Titles sometimes come first and guide us into the story. "What If" can give us a story when we look at a person or thing and wonder how that began or why he's that way or where it might head.

For *The Key for Spies*, my title came first, but it only gave me the necessity for a spy.

I didn't have Heyer's *An Infamous Army* in mind, not at all. Haunting me, though, was a desire to set a story in Spain. The Hearts in Hazard series demanded that the story fit in the Regency England time frame. Spain 1814 was controlled by Napoleon's France that had taken over the Spanish throne and garrisoned troops to control the country.

I needed a British spy, obviously working to overthrow French rule. The British spy would need help: Spanish guerrillas entered the story. I considered a female spy, but before she could touch a toe to the ground, the image of a Spanish lady shooting a pistol emerged. She emerge as Miriella Teba, reluctant leader of guerrillas.

Titles.

Character Requirements.

Character Inspiration.

Patterns set up elements that I want to use: tropes, motifs, recurring events in the series (such as dinner parties in every Hearts in Hazard title).

That's all that is necessary to start writing. Everything else is a gift from the creative muse.

AVOID OVER-PLANNING EACH SCENE.

I want an arc and the have-to elements. Even when I just start writing without a plan for the novel, I know I need conflict. I start considering a central antagonist. Minions develop, especially hidden ones, and then allies for my protagonist.

The antagonist of *The Key for Spies* doesn't really enter the story until chapter 5. When I started developing his voice, I backed up and wrote additional scenes, earlier insertions to fit what I already had.

His minions developed the same way.

The ally Chuy entered the story sketch as a betrayer, but by chapter 3 of the rough he had firmly decided on alliance and by chapter 12 he needed to become a voice in the story. That required more scenes at the beginning, insertions up to chapter 12, and brief plans through the rest of the story.

Characters will tell you what they need—when you listen.

Stories will tell you what they need—when you listen.

The rest of getting ideas for stories? Reaching a logical conclusion. Trying to add surprises. Research on details that sparks the unexpected.

I write and write. If the overnight sleep wakes me disgruntled, I re-consider the previous couple of days. During revision I re-consider.

Ideas come out of one story to create another. That germinal story seed may linger under soil for months. Occasionally it sprouts immediately.

The only given is to write every day. I may not reach my daily minimum word count, yet I keep writing.

Which feeds the creative muse > who gives ideas > which leads to more research > more surprises > more writing.

That's how I get my ideas.

Building a Book

Do you know the Number 1 indicator of writing success? Writing every day.

That incremental building of word counts incrementally builds a book.

And a completed book manuscript is what we're after. Disruptions and distractions occur and can be overcome all through writing every day.

To show you how a manuscript builds—and to show you how novels can be ever-expanding—I'm offering my word count tracking for a novel project that twisted me more than a few times from mid-May to early September. So, I'm tracking a single novel from its earliest glimmer of an idea to the publication end.

I've placed the tracking into a series of charts, set up in 10-day increments. Under each chart I have comments with analysis or frustration about any problems that occurred. As the charts reach their end, I share my original thinking about the fiction project and how that changed.

Hopefully, as you peruse the charts and my comments, you can analyze problems with completing your own writing projects and move past any stumbling blocks. You may find this especially helpful when I explain the reason behind certain skipped days.

In the Charts ~

Day needs no explanation.

Stage of Writing ~ I have 7 stages of writing.

Dividing your own writing process into stages helps you get through the massive undertaking that is a novel. A good metaphor is a tree. All the background that no one sees would be the roots. The basic foundation of characters and situation and setting is the sturdy trunk. The branches and limbs and leaves are the countless details that go into writing the novel. Then we have the birds and their nests, your distribution stream for your manuscript, whether you go the independent writer approach or follow the traditional publishing method.

Here are my stages.

1. Ideas = quickly writing brief notes
2. Sketch = the barest shape of a scene, occasionally with dialogue but usually only events. When I have around 20 scenes following a story arc (plot sequence, character arc), I place them into the Archetypal Story Pattern to see if they create a story. Gaps in the ASP means that I have more scenes to write. This can be frustrating as I try to create an interesting story. A sketch may be a half-page that will turn into 15 pages in the Rough. Very similar to an outline, but it flows one idea to the next and may skip entire scenes.

3. Rough = the shape of the story, scenes and sequels written as chapters, complete sentences, many but not all details. Some call this the "rough draft" or "first draft". In my mind, it's the story coming together for the first time. This is the most difficult stage of the 7, for this creates the first form of the novel.
4. Draft = the rough transformed into the novel. Details of character and setting and situation become elaborate. A finished draft is a completed manuscript. Writing a clean draft—without holes or gobbledygook such as *put something interesting here*—prevents the necessity of multiple drafts. Strive for a single draft. With the work in the Sketch and the Rough, the Draft is not difficult.
5. Proof-Plus = Revisions and editing, looking for plot holes and character discrepancies, adding motifs, clarifying details, removing over-writing. As a newbie, revisions may be massive. The most important thing to avoid is overwriting. Enhancement through motifs or the occasional sentence crafting (metaphors, etc.) occurs in this Stage—always keeping in mind the mantra to Avoid Overwriting.
6. Corrections = This two-step process incorporates everything from Proof-Plus. Then I generate a new print-out and work through the manuscript again, looking for typos and grammos. No one is 100% perfect, but I can try. Many eyes on the manuscript help spot these errors.
7. PUB / Publication & Promotion = Publication is getting the manuscript into a distribution chain (traditional or independent). A traditional writer sends the MS to agents and editors; an indie writer sends the book direct to a distributor such as Amazon or Ingrams or others. Trad writers also create a synopsis and query letter. The indie writer has to handle sub-contractors such as cover designers and editors. Both have in common the blurb or market copy, which is the teaser and usually part of the query letter. Promotions cover everything from blog posts to ads on platforms, video trailers and swag, and author pages on the distributor and review sites such as GoodReads.

When I first began writing, I had no stages. I just launched, re-worked constantly, and really had no idea what I was doing or where the manuscript was going. Several years ago, my 7 stages were Ideas / Shape / Draft / Revise / Enhance / Edit / Print. A couple of years after I began publishing I re-aligned the stages to match what I was actually doing and revised them to the 7 that I now use: Ideas / Sketch / Rough / Draft / Proof-Plus / Corrections / Publishing. All of the stages have additional tasks within them.

Chapter or Focus is another obvious area of the chart.

In my Sketch world, I am a pantster in puzzling behavior, which means that I may sketch out scenes at many different points in the novel, end before beginning, late middle before mid-middle, and that kind of thing. The Sketch follows my intuitive sense of story. After placing the scenes into the Archetypal Story Pattern, I usually do not have to write additional scenes. The ASP helps me know what part of the story may be missing.

In the Rough world, I am a pantster following a story's chronological progression, writing the book as a reader would see it. If I write a scene on one day then can't immediately start back on the next day, then I will pull out that scene and start writing from its beginning. Usually, I have missed a step which I will see during this second run at the scene. (I might have called it a re-write except that it's not a re-write, since the scene completely changes.)

In Drafting and afterward, I am a plotter in a chronological progression, sticking tightly to the story arc to ensure all scenes fit together and all sequels flow from scene to scene without disruptions. In Drafting a mystery, for example, I have to ensure enough real clues and red herrings are included for the reader.

The Word Count for a particular day is an estimate for the Rough Stage, accurate for Draft, an estimate for Proof-Plus (if given at all), and accurate for corrections. When a word count is listed for Ideas (rarely) and Sketch, then that is an estimate. All estimates are always conservative, casting *under* what the actual word count may be.

Total in Document = for the Rough and earlier Stages, this is an estimate. For the Draft and later Stages, this is an accurate word count. If I back up and insert scenes and other material in the Rough Stage, this number will run far below a close estimate.

Sometimes my Rough and Draft word counts are very similar. With this project, however, because I had so many insertions, the Rough under-estimated by about one-third of the final length. The number of insertions sent me into the Draft before the Rough was half-completed; the track of the story was getting jumbled in my mind. I usually wait until I am closer to the end of the Rough (last five to seven chapters) before I start the Draft.

For ease of management, the table is split month to month as well as in 10-day increments. For ease of reading, each table is on a separate page.

BEGINNING THE STORY IN APRIL

Day	Day Count	Stage of Writing	Pages written	Chapters or Focus	Word Count	Total in Document
Fri	1	1st Sketch		Protagonist in 1st danger	1,300	
	4/13			Working on a Fiction project		
Sun	2	Sketch		Opening ideas for main conflict, primary murder to be solved		
				The time between now and May 9 was focused on completing two projects: one fiction, one non-fiction.		

MAY

Day	Day Count	Stage of Writing	Pages written	Chapters or Focus	Word Count	Total in Document
Tues	3	Sketch		Very rough idea of scenes	1,192	
	4	Research		Background information		
	5	Ideas / Master Book		Character basics: appearance / GMC; side characters / setting		
	5/10			Working on a Non-Fiction project		

The Master Book is your book's Bible. It contains all sorts of factual information. You can make it as thick as you want or as slim.

If you plan to write a series, the Master Book is essential.

I had a one-off book for which I never intended to write a series. Six years later an idea for the sequel appeared. A Master Book would have saved my re-reading that first book.

MID-MAY

Day	Day Count	Stage of Writing	Pages written	Chapters or Focus	Word Count	Total in Document
Sat	6	Ideas				
Sun	7	Sketch			100	
Mon	8	Rough		Manuscript started	3,135	
Tues	9	Rough	21-27	Ch. 2 > 3	1,600	
Wed	10	Sketch			260	
Thu	11	Rough	28-35	Ch. 4 > 5	1,688	
Fri	12	Rough		Ch. 5 > 6	2,300	
Sat	13	Rough		Ch. 6 > 7	2,000	12,430 Rough
	5/19			Taken off for a family gathering		
Mon	14	Rough	56-64		1,780	

The table above displays the start of the actual manuscript.

I set a goal of 1,500 words per day for the Rough Stage. The benefit of the foundational work shows in the 1st, 4th and 5th days of the Rough stage. 7,435 words in three days with 3,288 on the other two days.

May's End

Day	Day Count	Stage of Writing	Pages written	Chapters or Focus	Word Count	Total in Document
Tues	15	Rough	64-68	Ch. 8 finished	942	
	16	Sketch			1,200	
Wed	17	Rough	69-77	Ch. 9	1,815	
Thu	18	Sketch			400	
Fri	19	Sketch			200	
Sat - Tues	5/25 -28			Ribs broken, with four days taken off because of pain		
Wed	20	Rough	79-95		3,930	
Thu	21	Rough		Inserting new backstory for one of the protagonists	1,000	
Fri	22	Rough	96-105	Ch. 12	2,025	

Breaking my ribs on Friday evening was a painful disruption.

For the first four days, all story writing was completely suspended—except in my head.

You can see the reward of the thinking on Wednesday and on Thursday. Those days away from the story not only gave me tons of ideas that boosted my word-count, including into the next week. The days away also gave me fresh ideas for one of my protagonists; his backstory and motivation and desired goal completely changed.

While that Wednesday was a great day, the next couple of months reveal the toll of the injury. My sleep for the next couple of months was ruined, and that deprivation shows up in additional days taken away from this project.

JUNE

Day	Day Count	Stage of Writing	Pages written	Chapters or Focus	Word Count	Total in Document
Sat	23	Rough	105-116	Ch. 13 > 14	2,550	
Sun	24	Rough	117-123	Ch. 14	1,575	
Mon	25	Rough	124-131	Ch. 15	1,900	
Tues	26	Rough	132-141	Ch. 16 > 17	2,600	
Wed	27	Rough	142-151	Ch. 17	2,100	
Thu	28	Rough	151-157	Ch. 18	1,800	
Fri	29	Rough	158-161	Ch. 19 started	1,050	
Sat	30	Rough	161-163	Ch. 19	750	
Sun	31	Rough	164-169	Ch. 19 > 20	2,100	
	6/10			Errands / Promotional Posts for July		

Chapter 19 was obviously a struggle. I didn't achieve my daily word count. Once I broke through the problem, however, the word count soared past the daily 1,500 minimum.

Mid-June

Day	Day Count	Stage of Writing	Pages written	Chapters or Focus	Word Count	Total in Document
Mon	31	Ideas		Ideas for a new voice		
Tues	33	Rough		Insertions for the new voice	2,043	
Wed	34	Ideas		More ideas for the new voice		
	6/14			Working on a Non-Fiction project		
Sat	35	Draft	1-16	Ch. 1 > 2	4,227	4,227 Draft
Sun	36	Draft	17-30	Ch. 2 > 3	4,699	4,699 D
Mon	37	Rough		Insertions for new voice	2,790	
Tues	38	Rough		Insertions for new voice	1,540	
Wed	39	Rough		Fixing and insertion for Ch. 20	1,675	
Thu	40	Rough	170-174	Ch. 20	1,125	

The new voice is a secondary character who began demanding his own scenes with his own point of view. I had resisted him for several days then gave in. He'll show up in the sequel to this book—and maybe his own series in the future. He's a character worthy of more books.

Those insertions required moving back into several places in the story. Gradually, after all these insertions, I began thinking the story was disjointed. To save myself, I began working on the Draft much earlier than I normally would have.

Working on the Draft at the same time as the Rough created additional problems. Twice I lost track of where I was working in the story. Once I had to return to a written scene to straighten out the time problems. The second time, I basically re-wrote the same scene but two days apart in the novel's timeline. That was another frustrating fix.

This issue of confusion (disjointed story and scene mix-ups) may have been the result of sleepiness from the pain caused by broken ribs. I have had similar insertions in previous manuscripts without these problems.

The Non-Fiction project is a slow build. I use one day each week to work on it. I missed the previous two weeks, and the three weeks before I just crowded the work in after this project writing for the day.

JUNE'S END

Day	Day Count	Stage of Writing	Pages written	Chapters or Focus	Word Count	Total in Document
	6/21 to 25			Three days on Non-Fiction Project. One day = family celebration. One other day without any work.		
Wed	41	Draft	31-41	Ch. 4	4,451	13,377 D
Thu	42	Blurb		Market Copy	250	
		Rough	175-183 + page 191	Ch. 21 > 22		50,000 R
Fri	43	Blurb		Re-thinking the Market Copy	351	
		Trailer		Using the Trailer to Fix the Blurb	1,000	
Sat	44	Draft	to p. 47	Ch. 5	2,324	15,701 D
	6/30			Nothing		

In this set of 10 days, I have only four days on this project, one of which is actually not *on* the manuscript. It's great to complete a manuscript and have the blurb completed, but it's disruptive to completing the manuscript itself.

Just when you think the pain and sleeplessness should be over, it's not. The pain injections are wearing off, and the over-the-counter pain medications aren't reducing my pain levels.

June 21 to 25 were difficult. I can manage non-fiction writing when I can't manage fiction; the creative muse needs sleep in order to offer writing ideas. Only one day of this five is totally lost. The other day was a family celebration. You can't miss those!

Then June 30 is a second total miss in this 10-day span.

Check out the next week. I can blame the July 4th disruption only on the 4th. What happened on the other days?

JULY

Day	Day Count	Stage of Writing	Pages written	Chapters or Focus	Word Count	Total in Document
Mon	45	Rough	193-201	Ch. 23	2,300	
	7/2			Promotions for July and August		
Wed	46	Draft	48-55 + 60	Ch. 6 > 7	5,103	20,804 D
	7/4			Independence Day celebration		
	7/5			Working on a Non-Fiction project		
Sat	47	Draft	61-69	Ch. 8	3,243	24,047 D
	7/7-10			Nothing		

3 days out of 10 on this fiction project—plus one day off for Independence Day and one day on the slow-burn non-fiction project and one day on promotions. Thus, five good days out of 10 plus one celebration day.

But four days lost, all in a row.

Mid-July

Day	Day Count	Stage of Writing	Pages written	Chapters or Focus	Word Count	Total in Document
	7/11			Nothing		
Fri	48	Rough			1,800	
Sat	49	Draft	70-94	Ch. 9, 10, & 11	7,604	32,820 D
	7/14-15			Nothing		
Tues	50	Rough	174B-H	Insertion of new chapter	1,850	
Wed	51	Rough	to 175	Insertion of new chapter (9 pages)	2,400	
	7/18			Work on Nonfiction project and an upcoming presentation for a writers' group		
Fri	52	Draft	95-99	Ch. 12 started	1,606	34,426 D
Sat	53	Draft	99-103	Ch. 12	1,810	36,266 D

This set of 10 days has 6 writing days and a single working day—7 out of 10 good days. Improving, but not at the previous rate.

Three days are on the Draft when I need to finish the Rough. Is it avoidance? Or the accumulating sleep deprivation because the pain is only slowly abating?

Also in this set of 10 days, I began realizing that I would blow past my original word count goal for the novel. I wanted 55,000 words. The Rough has more than 5 chapters to go and will probably hit 30 chapters. The insertion are scenes needed that I didn't previously realize.

In this week I admitted that this would be a long book.

Last year I struggled through a long book in the horrid hot months of summer. That project began in May, went nowhere in June and July, picked up in August, then started going at a good pace in October. I finished that book in January, which means that the project took 8 ½ months to write.

On the 20th, seeing the Draft run at 36,000-plus words, I knew that I would probably top 75,000 words, a half-longer than anticipated. *Yikes*, I was thinking, but I still followed where the story led rather than cutting it short.

This is the glory of self-publishing. An Ivory Tower doesn't control the castle I'm building.

July's End

Day	Day Count	Stage of Writing	Pages written	Chapters or Focus	Word Count	Total in Document
Sun	54	Draft	103-112	Ch. 12 > 13	3,984	40,220
Mon	55	Draft	113-117	Ch. 13 finished	1,808	42,028 D
	7/23			Nothing		
Wed	56	Draft	118-128	Ch. 14 (11 p.)	4,309	46,337 D
	7/25			Nothing		
Fri	57	Draft	129-137	Ch. 15 > 16	3,118	49,455 D
	7/27 -28			Organizing and work on Non-Fiction Project		
	7/29			Promotions for September		
Tues	58	Rough	174-184		1,140	
Wed	59	Draft	136-143 + 3	Ch. 16 finished	3,287	52,742

This is an 11-day span. I have focused on the biz on 6 + 3 days, 9 of the 11.

The Plus 3 are working on other writing biz. Only two days have no writing at all. Improving, but still not where I want to be.

AUGUST

Day	Day Count	Stage of Writing	Pages written	Chapters or Focus	Word Count	Total in Document
	8/1			Work on Non-Fiction Project		
Fri	60	Draft	144-152	Ch. 17	3,359	56,281 D
	8/3 -4			Creative Muse forces new project		
Mon	61	Sketch		7 pages	1,575	
		Rough		8 pages	2,200	
Tues	62	Draft	153-164	Ch. 18	4,189	60,470 D
Wed	63	Draft	165-168	Ch. 19 started	1,466	61,936 D
	8/8			Creative Muse Project		
Fri	64	Draft	169-174	Ch. 19 finished	2,202	64,138 D
	8/10			Creative Muse Project		

This is a great first 10 days of August! I'm working every day. The Draft is catching up to the Rough. I need to move forward with the Rough, yet my focus remains the Draft.

The Draft will also run much higher than my 2nd anticipated length of 75,000 words.

Check the word count difference. I'm receiving more reward from the Draft. Sketching and Roughing out a story is much more difficult than extending actions/opinions to their proper length along with elaborating details and firming up problems in the story.

In this 10-day span, only half of the days are devoted to this project. I have a writing distraction I'm pursuing. I tried to avoid it, but by Saturday it pressed hard for completion.

I know what's happening, though—the creative muse needs to distract the critical mind while she focuses on completing the last chapters of this manuscript. That's what happened on Monday in this chart: the muse came through with the Sketch and the Rough on one day > 3,775 new words in one day.

How do we judge whether we should pursue a distracting project? Here's the answer. 1] I'm still returning to this novel project. 2] The new project, non-fiction, fits into my writing business plan, so I'll let it play out. 3] Self-publishing allows me to back up the publication deadline for this project. My creative muse will have the time she needs to figure the ending out.

MID-AUGUST

Day	Day Count	Stage of Writing	Pages written	Chapters or Focus	Word Count	Total in Document
Sun	65	Draft	175-187	Ch. 20	4,679	68,817 D
Mon	66	Sketch		4 pages / Muse at Work	880	
Tues	67	Draft	188-197	Ch. 21	3,472	72,289 D
	8/14 -16			Creative Muse Project / one day on the other NF project		
Sat	68	Rough	213-219 + 3	Ch. 27 > 28 / Muse at Work	2,250	63,800 R
Sun	69	Rough	220-228	Ch. 28 > 30 (Ch. 29 already written) / Muse at Work	2,250	
	8/19 -20			Creative Muse Project		

Another great week: working on projects every day. The Creative Muse Project is taking three days this span, four days last span, and three more days in the next span, but then it's done, almost as if it helped serve as a bridge to return me to focusing on a single project.

Look at the total word counts on Tuesday for the Draft and Saturday for the Rough. It's futile to keep tracking the word count for the Rough while the Draft (at seven chapters back) has blown past that number. Right now, I'm tracking the amount to see how much the insertions added. Scenes came in for one of the protagonists and then for a character moving from secondary to sub-primary.

I have definitely mis-calculated the insertion word counts.

Letting the Muse work, however, is showing a pay-off in this set of 10 days. I'm so close to the end, the glowing light is blinding.

Come on, Muse! Do your work faster! The Draft is rushing forward like a mighty wind.

AUGUST'S END

Day	Day Count	Stage of Writing	Pages written	Chapters or Focus	Word Count	Total in Document
Wed	70	Draft	197-205	Ch. 22	3,386	75,675 D
Thu	71	Blurb		Checked		
		Draft	206-212	Ch. 23	2,407	78,082 D
	8/23 -25			Creative Muse Project / last three days		
Mon	72	Draft	213-231	Ch. 24 > 25	6,866	84,948 D
Tues	73	Rough	229-247	Ch. 31 > 32 / Rough is Finished!	5,500	70,395 R
Wed	74	Draft	232-250	Ch. 26 > 27	6,881	91,827 D
Thu	75	Draft	251-275	Ch. 28 > 30	7,919	99,748 D
Fri	76	Draft	275-295	Ch. 30 > 32 / Draft is Finished!	6,953	106,701 D
Sat	77	Proof-Plus		Prologue to MidPoint		

The muse did her work. The Rough finished in one day, far more than the original 55,000 projected and far less than the actual word count.

The Creative Muse Project distracted the conscious brain just enough that she could do her creative work and have the necessary twists and surprises for the last chapters.

The Blurb, written much earlier because of sleep deprivation, is checked to ensure the teaser matches to the story on the page.

I originally had a deadline of July 15, backed that up to July 30 then August 15, and finally Aug. 31. I didn't make August 31 as the publication date, but it will be close.

As I feared, this novel will run double the projected length once the Back Matter promotional material about other books is added.

298 total pages with the Notes (snippets about information, such as lock picking).

26 days to write the Rough / 25 days for the Draft / other days not counted. Close to 107,000 words in 76 days ~ that's excellent.

FINISHING IN SEPTEMBER

Day	Day Count	Stage of Writing	Pages written	Chapters or Focus	Word Count	Total in Document
Sun	78	Proof-Plus		Mid-Point to End + Notes		
Mon	79	Corrections		Corrections beginning to end		
				Back Matter added		
		Published!			2,485	109,183 in the final document
		ISBN assigned				
		Copyright applied for				

And now promotions will begin!

Promotions include ~

- Video trailer for use on three different websites in addition to social media outlets
- Also on websites and social media outlets, these posts ~
  - Cover Reveal
  - Buy Link
  - Meet the female protagonist / Buy Link
  - Meet the male protagonist / Buy Link
  - Meet the sub-primary character who demanded his own scenes. (Sometimes, this would be a "meet the antagonist" post.) / Buy Link
- Ads on distribution outlets. (Social media outlet ads haven't worked as well.)

Deadline Match-Up

How far off from the original deadline of July 15 am I? Original Goal missed by 47 days.

Part of missing that original deadline was the injury. While I missed a few days right after I broke my ribs, I can't lay that 47-day delay on the injury alone. Sleep deprivation from pain definitely caused problems. How much I will never know.

Had the word count stayed at 55,000 as I anticipated when I began writing on Monday, May 13, then the Rough would have been there very quickly after June 27, ahead of the deadline. The Draft achieved 55,000 on August 2, 18 days after the deadline, not too far off. Five of those days between June 27 and August 2 were working on the Rough; however, multiple days in that span were completely missed. Again, I blame the sleep deprivation.

The Creative Muse Project took 10 of those over-run days, but I believe that project helped finish this fiction project. Fiction requires creative ideas. You can't force them. While the muse dances around a maypole of ideas, you can use the time to work on other projects. Pick different kinds of projects. Fiction and Fiction doesn't work for me, but Fiction and NonFiction does. When your fiction muse becomes stumped, try working on a nonfiction project or on promotions. You'll quickly discover that Writer's Block doesn't exist; it's just your creative muse being impish.

So, original goal missed by 47 days.

10 of those were on a non-fiction project = 37.

12 days were on a slow-build NF project or were writing biz-related = 25.

3 days were for family celebrations (including Fireworks!) = 22.

15 days were because of pain and sleep deprivation = 7.

Only seven days truly behind. That doesn't look so bad.

When you think you're not accomplishing very much, here are 3 things to do.

1st > Make a list of everything that you have accomplished since you first committed yourself to your writing goal. Commitment is a key. Commitment requires you to have a daily, achievable word count. Sometimes writing every day is simply not possible. Mine is 1,500 words per day, but sometimes I drop that count depending on life rolls. If you can only do 500 words, that is still more than nothing!

2nd > Using the power of increments, decide how many days you will need to complete your current project. How many words do you think the project will need? How many days each week can you squeeze 500 words? (Or the word count that you can achieve?) Set aside one day each week for no writing. Yes, I'm serious about this. If you write on that day, great, but you won't feel guilty if you miss one day each week. When you use it, flip that day out with a missed day. See? No stress.

3rd > Once you know the number of days, start tracking. Track anything writing related. Label it based on the stage of writing. Try to achieve your word count goal PLUS a little more. And watch your project build, increment by increment, until you have Built a Book.

INDEX

LISTED > BE A WRITER ~ 13 STEPS FOR DANCING

1] Just start writing.

2] Be certain of your peeps.

3] Use patterns and models.

4] Be a pro with the manuscript.

5] Be willing to lose control.

6] Be twisty with plot.

7] Be willing to have minor antagonists.

8] Be global with an antagonist.

9] Be angsty.

10] Use surprise.

11] Be disciplined with writing.

12] Be a tracker.

13] Be a friend to jot lists.

LISTED > INTO THE LABYRINTH ~ 10 BITS OF STRING

1] Keep writing. Writers have more than one story to tell.

2] A single character can give several novels.

3] Pay attention to what the character and the story need.

4] Finish what you start. Without listening to other people's comments. Those comments can kill your story.

5] First Readers only read finished manuscripts.

6] No matter how hard the book is, never throw anything away.

7] Pay attention to the world around you.

8] Never be daunted.

9] A story will tell you want it needs.

10] Don't let the past hang over you.

LISTED > INTO WONDERLAND

Rule 1 :: Never stop.

Rule 2 :: Work professionally.

Rule 3 :: First attractors to books are the covers.

Acknowledgements :: Kin and kith are most important.

Write a Book in a Month

Inspiration 4 Writers ~ 2

by Remi Black

Introduction

Last April I gave myself a dare. I wanted to write a novella, about 30,000 words. I decided to log my success and failures as an open blog for other writers. The result it this: *Write a Book in a Month*.

I didn't have a steady record of 30,000 words in a month. In the previous year, I needed eight+ months to write 96,000 words. That works out to be 12,000 words a month. It's actually 24,000 words on average that came through my fingers per month. I do a complete Rough and a complete Draft as separate documents: the rough hand-written and the draft onto computer.

Handwriting the Rough gives me permission to scratch out mistakes, to fly through scenes, and to slog through problems.

Still, the previous high point of 24,000 words is far short of the 30,000 challenge goal. Not counted in that word count were these Daily Logs.

I set myself this challenge because I needed the push to stay disciplined with my writing.

Come along to see how well I did and benefit from each day's lesson.

APRIL 1 ~ NO FOOLING

Current Project :: *To Wield the Wind*
Project Stage :: Sketching Ideas
Today's Word Count: 200
Total Word Count: 5,920 / 33,000
Goal: 5,000 words per week
Weekly Words Achieved 200
Project Dates: March 25 to May 5 Publication

These blogs are a day-by-day account of my writing time, along with method and focus as well as everything that interferes and distracts from my goal. Sometimes I will have a lot to say; some days, not so much.

The goal is 1,000 words per working day, with 5,000 words as the weekly goal. I want to write for 30 straight days, then Proof Plus for 10, and publish on the 10th day.

How did I arrive at this daily and weekly word count as my goal? The 4 Bees:

1. Be realistic. Don't push for what I wish, but for what I can do.
2. Be time-aware. Use writing time wisely. Find places in the day to achieve the goal.
3. Be devoted. Stick to the one fiction project. Keep focused throughout the day on achieving the daily goal.
4. Be specific. Know what I'm doing, when I'm doing it, why, and how.

The 4 Bees are today's Lesson 1.

Realistic goals are key. I spent the first three months of this year burning through three projects for a different pseudonym. In January I completed a 96,000-word book started last May. On February 28 I published a 60,000-word book. March saw the publication of a slow-build nonfiction project.

Burning through creative projects will quickly burn me out. Since I'm tackling a third fiction project at the same time that I write these 30 nonfiction blogs, I need to ease up just a little on the fiction side. Instead of pushing for 2500+ words per writing day, as I did in January and February, I'm going for 1,000+ wpd. I will achieve more wpd than 1,000, but I'm not counting the wpd for these blogs.

Why did I pick 5,000 words per week? I jumbled up business and creativity. *No fooling*.

Whenever writers start a project, they need to have very good creative *and* business reasons.

Business and Creativity are odd companions for writers. We need the first; we thrive on the second. We have to learn to work with both together.

If you haven't yet done so, you need to create a Business Plan for yourself, projecting from where you are now to where you want to be five years from now. This is Lesson 2 for today.

- Vision: the image of where you want your business to be in five years
- Mission: the niche filled with your writing, the focus that will make your writing different from other writers of similar stories
- Objectives: concrete goals that prove you are fulfilling your vision
- Strategies: specific methods to help you achieve each concrete goal.
- Plans: pull out a calendar and start drafting your seasonal, monthly, and weekly plans that will complete each strategy and goal.

So, what did I do today? I didn't plan to write at all. No fooling, even though it's April Fool's Day.

I planned to take off the day because I only took one day for myself during the entire month of March. Remember what I said earlier? Burning through projects can quickly burn you out. I self-published a book in January, a second in February, and a third in March.

Today I ran errands. I cooked. I cleaned. I played some games on my phone.

But the work that I'd accomplished last week called to me, giving me ideas for this upcoming week. So, in extremely rough form, across 10 index cards, I sketched out several ideas. I had tinkered with this story a little bit last summer, when things weren't going well with the 96,000-word opus. I had about 5,700 words written, the opening chapter with its problem.

This is Lesson 3. If you have several ideas flood over you, scribble them down. You don't need to write them neatly. They just have to be readable. They don't even have to be organized.

I know that I wrote more than 20 words per card, but a conservative estimate of wpd is 200. That's what I'm recording. That's what I'm telling you. With no fooling.

April 2 ~ Change of Plans

Current Project :: *To Wield the Wind*
Project Stage :: Rough Shape
Today's Word Count: 1,760
Total Word Count: 7,680 / 33,000
Goal: 5,000 words per week
Weekly Words Achieved 1,960
Project Dates: March 25 to May 5 Publication

Writers constantly evolve their process even as they hark back to their earliest days as a writer and especially as they hark back to failures.

The process should evolve. When things aren't working, switch it up. Give a new method three or four days. If it's not working, try another. And another. Until you hit one where the words will flow once you're about 7 minutes into the day's writing.

For April, I'm writing my next Remi Black.

This is a drastic change of plan. I had *planned* to write the next in the Alstera series, *To Wield a Fae-sharpened Sword* followed by *To Kindle a Dragon's Fire* and *Dance to Bone-Edged Music*. However. . . .

Writers have to look long-term, and Remi Black is a pseudonym that I want to ride long-term. That's Lesson 5.

Remi needs some help.

What kind of help? Draw-ins. If that's a word. It's definitely the answer.

Patty Jansen gives new writers excellent advice in her three-part series *Self-Publishing Unboxed*. One bit that she advises, basically, is not becoming too tied to one world. She describes her method: Write a trilogy and put it up, write another unrelated trilogy, write a third. While writing a fourth trilogy, see which series is catching on, and write another book for it.

Most self-publishers write an early book, shorter than others which gives a taste of the world they've built. They push this short book out to readers, through an email list or a Book Funnel or a freebie or cheap price. The purpose is to lure in readers with the first book and hope they continue with the series. The short book is called the *loss-leader*.

The loss-leader only works with a back-list, which is other longer novels at a higher price.

I'm three novels into the Enclave series. All three novels are over 100,000. Time and length remove them from the running as a loss-leader.

Time to write a loss-leader for the Enclave series.

Loss-leaders need to have connections to the other books in the series. For some books, finding a connected character to drive the story is relatively easy.

Yet I wanted to change the tone of the books and find a character with straightforward issues.

I started thinking about all of this months ago. Lesson 6 is that you need to gather up ideas and let them swirl around before you act on them. The results will be richer than what you would have jumped into.

Yesterday, I discussed business and creativity, odd companions for the writer. In considering the loss-leader, I jumbled up both and let the need steep for a while.

Business ~ I need to write another Enclave book; it's been a year since the last one was published. This summer I have deadlines for other books (under a different pseudonym) which means no time for that Enclave book, which takes three times as long as the books for the other pseudonym. Deciding to write a loss-leader to help more people find the series was one part of the business decision.

Bundling three books is another business decision. People like deals. Book-bundling can offer several books at a lower price, offering them "on sale". Three books tied together could easily be bundled. Three short books bundled together can be the length of the other Enclave books.

Creativity ~ The Enclave series forms an epic with a somber tone. Last year, my creative muse started erupting ideas with brighter tones (which are a definite indication of my happier life). The muse dreamed up the idea of the Enclave World. I should have been working on another book, but I was struggling. To help me, the muse launched a couple of other stories, giving me something to dream about while I worked through the issues that were slowing the other book down. I worked through a lot of the Foundation and Visioning stages for the story and then sketched a few scenes.

About six weeks ago—as I finished one book and launched into the next *and* realized that I needed another Remi Black—the muse said, "Look. Here. I've given you the answer already. I'm a prophet." She said the last very smugly.

Business & Creativity ~

- Connection ~ I'm writing the first of three short books with a third-level character from the original Enclave series.
- Tone ~ The Enclave World books will have a lighter tone.
- Length ~ Novellas should run from 30,000 to 35,000. Bundled, that's 110,000 words.
- Project ~ About 1,000 words for 30 days.

Biz goal determined. Creativity spiked. I get to play with *To Wield the Wind*.

Change of plans launched.

April 3 ~ Stick with the Plan

Current Project :: *To Wield the Wind*
Project Stage :: Sketching Ideas
Today's Word Count: 1,100
Total Word Count: 8,780 / 33,000
Goal: 5,000 words per week
Weekly Words Achieved 3,060
Project Dates: March 25 to May 5 Publication

When things are working, we grab onto our method and let the words flow. When things aren't working, we have to switch things around.

How do we know when things aren't working? The words won't come.

That sounds simple. It's not.

A lot of things can interfere with our writing goals. Lack of exercise. Bad food habits. Commitments, obligations, distractions. Stress from work. Stress at home. Some days, we need the good Lord just to cope with life.

Writing can be an escape from all that.

For many years, that's all it truly is. We love stories. We read to escape. The muse gives us ideas, and we start tinkering with them. Then running with those ideas. Until the sparkling new is rubbed off and the story becomes as difficult as life. That's when we decide to pursue the next new sparkling shiny.

Monday, I wrote 200 words on my newest project, *To Wield the Wind*. 200 words is not many. It's 200 more than I planned to write.

You see, I wrote for 30 days of the 31 available during March. In February, I wrote for 25 of the available 28. In January, I wrote for 25 of the available 31. I've written 80 days this year, and it's only the start of April. I've never achieved this high number at the three-month mark.

Want more numbers? In January, over 70,000 words flowed through my fingers. In February, over 70,000. In March, over 70,000. Over 210,000 words. That sounds improbable until you realize that the number is only 2,625 words for each of the 80 days.

I *wanted* to write that much. I enjoyed every one of those 80 days of writing.

But it's intensive, isn't it? Remembering how intensive those three months were, I understand the need to back off.

Back off—or be backed off.

I would rather choose my stoppages. Not burned out and never knowing when the goals train will start up again.

So the April plan will follow more realistic goals. 1,000 words is two 5-paragraph essays. That's doable. That length on a good day is at two hours; on a bad day, that's closer to four hours.

Commitments occur in April. Spring itself is a HUGE distraction. Factor in days off from writing every week. Use them to recover lost time.

I'm already ahead. Lucky me! I finished the last book early, so I launched this one on Monday, March 25. I've mulled over *To Wield the Wind* for several months, after working on the Foundation and Visioning stages last summer. This story provided an escape for about three months, until the other book came together.

That's two of the lessons for *Stick with the Plan*. Lesson 7 Keep slogging at the novel that's coming slowly. Lesson 8 Get joy by exploring another project. Then I figured out the problems with the other book and returned to an intensive focus on it. Lesson 9: When the words are flowing, focus intensively on one creative project.

So, *WWind* started on March 25. By March 30 I had 5,720 words. The first week's goal achieved.

I could rest back on my heels and count the extra 720 words as part of this week. I won't, though. That's Lesson 10. Keep meeting the realistic goal. Keep following the plan. Keep writing 1,000 words for five days of every week.

Monday's 200 words were sketched ideas. That's Lesson 11. Use one of the off days to think about upcoming scenes.

Tuesday was 760 over a very good day with few interruptions, great focus, and free-flowing words. I may need to count these extra words to achieve this week's goal. Company's coming. That means house to clean and cooking to do. Cooking means errands to run.

Today, I focused on my usual Wednesday commitments, both for writing and for life. I have 1,100 words for today.

I *Stick with the Plan*, and I'm watching the novel build, one increment at a time.

APRIL 4 ~ NIX DISTRACTIONS

Current Project :: *To Wield the Wind*
Project Stage :: Sketching Ideas
Today's Word Count: 1,364
Total Word Count: 10,144 / 33,000
Goal: 5,000 words per week
Weekly Words Achieved 4,424
Project Dates: March 25 to May 5 Publication

Distractions, commitments, and obligations are a writer's bane. Commitments are to family and friends. Obligations are necessaries, like jobs and paying bills. And doing taxes. You know the tax man is coming, don't you?

Let me tell you about this week.

We can't stop the commitments and obligations. We have to plan for as many of them as possible.

Distractions, though—distractions we have to nix.

Today is the perfect example of a distraction. Today started with the knowledge that company's coming, so I had to get ready for them.

I had to cook. I had to clean. I got all of that out of the way with two hours to spare. The two hours that I would need for writing. I thought, "I can squeeze in my writing before they arrive. Two hours. I'll set the timer." I cleared off my workspace, put bum in chair (BiC can sometimes be the most difficult part of daily writing). Picked up my pen to start my jot list—and they arrived.

Two hours early!

Nevertheless, I managed to get in 1,364 words in a little less than a couple of hours, after everyone else went to bed. I'll be a little groggy tomorrow, but that's okay. I don't expect to write tomorrow.

How did I manage to achieve 1,364 words?

First, I knew what I was going to write. That's Lesson 12 for today.

Whenever I end a writing session, I list about 7 upcoming things that will happen next: upcoming conflict, action sequence, dialogue, character emotions, anything that's swirling that still needs to be written.

Lesson 13: Never write until you're dry. Always end with ideas for the next scene(s).

So the jot list became my start list. I rewrote it, adding ideas that had come up.

My jot list for today is still to come. I wanted to write this blog before I did the list. Which leads me to . . .

Lesson 14: A little distance helps to firm up ideas. A few minutes can grow a single word into sentences, an image into a paragraph, a few hasty thoughts into a stream of scenes. You just have to scribble them down in a readable handwriting.

Lesson 15: Keep sketched ideas handy. Those sketched ideas from Monday were still available as well as all of the Foundation and Visioning work from last summer. The work from several months ago was growing new ideas even as it started to morph away from the original root stock.

Lesson 16: Keep writing.

That is what this blog is about: overcoming distractions so we can keep writing.

Yesterday, the major distraction was the major one of dog-sitting. I crowded in my writing after little Bosco left, after I was tired—because he's a fireball of fun and exhaustion that I love. But I managed 1,100 words.

Tuesday was a good day, not squeezed in writing, no distractions. 1,760 words.

Monday I didn't intend to write at all, but I wound up writing 200 unexpected words, mostly sketched ideas—ideas that saved today.

Writers have to do this. On the days that we plan to write, we can't just take off. We have to know we're going to achieve the week's goal before we even consider taking a day off. And when we're not actively writing, we're mulling over characters and plot and settings and conflicts and descriptions and story arcs and much, much more.

We are constantly looking ahead, planning for our commitments and obligations. Even when writing consistently, we have to factor in time for our personal lives, like family celebrations and social organizations and paying our own bills. We have to factor in time to take care of the business side of writing.

I have some volunteer writing that I do, which takes a couple of hours every Monday or Tuesday because the deadline is Wednesday 9 a.m.

I have an obligation tomorrow, company to send off, and bills to pay for April. I have a stinking feeling that Spring has sprung, and my family is going to want to spring it on me on Saturday morning.

I don't expect any writing on Friday—but who knows? I might get some ideas. They come in handy.

I know that I need 600 more words. Whether I get them Saturday or Sunday doesn't matter, as long as I finish them before Midnight Sunday.

So I'm off to make my list for the next writing session, then I'll turn in.

April 5 ~ Watch for Warnings

Current Project :: *To Wield the Wind*
Project Stage :: Sketching Ideas
Today's Word Count: 0,000
Total Word Count: 10,144 / 33,000
Goal: 5,000 words per week
Weekly Words Achieved 4,424
Project Dates: March 25 to May 5 Publication

Today I didn't expect to write. This blog is not "writing". I find nonfiction incredibly easy. After years upon years of teaching students how to write logical essays and writing practice essays with them and in advance of them, I can let the nonfiction words flow.

Fiction is harder. It takes creativity as well as logic. Creativity is hard, especially when your brain is drained. As my brain is drained today.

Today, I'd like to take you back to 2013, when I realized I could jump into indie publishing. I might as well. The whole purpose of *Write a Book in a Month* is to provide you several lessons about writing. My journey provides a lot of lessons about failures that drive success.

2013. Almost six full years ago. I can write a cargo ship with stuffed containers about piddling away my time, being unfocused on manuscripts, procrastinating and wasting time, all through that year.

My goals were too nebulous. "I want to publish my writing" is too vague. What writing? When? How to publish it? How to prepare it for publication? How to decide when it's finished and ready for preparation?

Whole tanker containers of what I didn't know that I should have known and have subsequently learned—all of these fill my two books for newbie and gonnabee writers. Those books are *Think like a Pro* and *Discovering Your Novel*. They contain the lessons that I learned from 2013 and onward. Don't make the mistakes that I did.

There. That's about all that is important for 2013.

In 2014, I decided to get serious—but I didn't really change my life to devote myself to my dream until the latter part of the year. September ushered those changes in. I went from playing at writing to writing four days a week, at minimum. I stopped whining about needing long blocks of time and used the hour or two available in the evenings. When the weekends came, I tried to get in four hours either

Saturday or Sunday. I thought I was doing well to hit 122 days of writing for the year.

I *thought* I was doing well.

My business plan—see how smart I was becoming? I knew to pay attention to the seminar courses entitled Business of Writing (Lesson 17). So, I set up a business plan to begin publishing the very next year.

My first book went up for sale in August 2015. Yippee! Deadline achieved. Then I published three books on the same day in October. I thought that would be a smart marketing ploy. By the end of 2015, I had written for 163 days. Four books out, one Edie Roones and three M.A. Lee. Goals met: check.

I didn't know what goals were.

That lesson was learned in 2016. The goal: five titles. That should be simple enough. I had manuscripts in drawers waiting to be refreshed. I would refresh three, write a couple.

I started the year by pulling out a short story that I sold for first print rights. I would publish under my Edie Roones pseudonym as first electronic rights. I wouldn't change it, not at all.

That would be my first publication for 2016.

"A Matter of Trust" served as a warning which I ignored.

You likely wonder why I am talking about all these past years of writing. They contain lots of lessons. Every time that I sit down to write, I remember all the way back to 2013. My mistakes in pursuing my goals, the distractions that pulled me away, the obstacles that tried to explode my dream--I remember all of those whenever I put bum in chair = Lesson 18.

I still make mistakes; no one can avoid that. I still encounter distractions; they will always occur. I fight the obstacles; they won't bring me down.

The goals that I now make are for daily, not monthly or yearly. They are achievable, not chalked marks that can be erased and re-set = Lesson 19.

"A Matter of Trust" served as a warning in 2016 for one simple reason: it should have been published before the 10th of January. It published 30 days later, on February 9.

Why was it a warning? Why does it remain a lesson for me?

Think about that ~ January 1 to February 9. Think how many days that is. I wasn't really doing anything else. If the short story would be my first publication, why wasn't I focusing on it?

2016 was a learning year. It was a year of failures. It was also a year of successes.

- A social media presence was necessary for a viable writing career. I started that = Success.

- Unfortunately, I did so by hiring someone to set up the website = Failure. I could have set up the website by myself—and I would have been happier with the end result. The designer had a major grammatical error on the home page. What I gave her didn't have the grammatical error. I'm an English teacher, high school and college. I have a Master of Arts and a Bachelor of Arts in English. Mistakes happen, but errors shouldn't occur. And when I took over the website, maintaining it wasn't as hard as I expected it to be. Yes, it took four days to re-build it, but still—.

- I wrote blogs on a regular basis. Success: I created my own content, strong content that I could use later for a nonfiction book.

- Failure: I spent too much time on writing and planning and researching blogs, rather than the fiction that would be my bread-and-butter.

- I looked up in March and had completed very little on the fiction. Failure: I needed to be working on my fiction.

- Success: I had blogs set up for three months away. Posting blogs well in advance became my watchword. And I could use them later, remember, for a nonfiction book. By the end of the year, I had 154 usable blogs.

Continuing in this way wasn't going to work. Even my job was especially horrendous, consuming hours beyond the workday. However, I was managing stress better. And I took a long trip to Canada, knocking out two long-term goals—returning to Quebec and exploring the eastern provinces. Failure. Failure. Success. Success.

Keep up with your failures and your successes. Write them down. You won't learn from the failures if they slip from memory. You won't recall the successes when you try to judge if you're succeeding. Track both. = Lesson 20.

I finished 2016 with 259 days of writing, 71% of the year. But too many of those days were blogs only. The blogs would have to come second to the fiction writing, even with the goal of writing nonfiction from them. Also, in 2016 only three fiction works were published, one of which was merely typing onto my laptop then uploading. So, only two books written, one for M.A. Lee and one for Edie Roones and one short story, previously written. Lots of blogs, though.

2017 was filled with Major Life Rolls. That's the focus for Saturday—because as I earlier suspected, sprung Spring is calling family and writing won't happen. I talked about anticipating distractions, didn't I?

Thank the good Lord that I only need to get 600 more words for this week.

APRIL 6 ~ LIFE ROLLS

Current Project :: *To Wield the Wind*
Project Stage :: Sketching Ideas
Today's Word Count: 0,000
Total Word Count: 10,144 / 33,000
Goal: 5,000 words per week
Weekly Words Achieved 4,424
Project Dates: March 25 to May 5 Publication

I had two major life rolls in 2017.

I planned for the life rolls. I was excited about them. I just didn't plan for the disruption that would cause in my writing = Lesson 21.

1] I left a job that I did extremely well but was causing stress and health issues that I just would no longer tolerate.

2] I moved, getting away from people who kept trying to pull me back into that job. The move put me closer to family and true friends (rather than friendly colleagues and friends of common worlds). I moved closer to mountains that inspire me, and I tried to learn to relax.

In 2017 I published three novels in the early part of the year. I started writing the first one in November 2016. The other two were sketched out and roughed into shape in December 2016. So I spent January, February, March and April writing then publishing these novels. I published the third on April 9.

I published a nonfiction book in May. I had tinkered with this book for several years. That NF book came together easily and quickly during April while I reviewed my plans for my first Remi Black, *To Weave a Wizardry Web*.

For the rest of 2017, I planned to write four more novels, one of which would merely be an update of old manuscript. I thought I would accomplish my goals, no problem. I was now writing full-time. I could do this!

Weave a Wizardry Web had given me trouble for years. I knew the arc for each of the dual main characters. I knew that I would need the perspectives of two other characters, which turned them into subprimes (if that makes sense). I had scenes scattered throughout the dual arcs, some of which I had up to six versions for. I just needed to put all of it together.

As soon as the third novel was published on April 9, I started running into trouble. I worked out the first problems before May started, took off a little time to finish up the NF book, then turned to focus on *Web*.

I hit the first life roll at the end of May.

And fell into the second life roll in mid-June. I moved. I went from a 3 BR house to an area the size of a small studio. I still had my house to sell. I had to deal with distractions from people I truly care for. I had to change my writing schedule.

Yet *Weave a Wizardry Web* started talking to me.

When story talks to a writer, that's a good thing. Writers have to listen. Lesson 22.

Web was supposed to published in July. It published August 2. "Okay," I said to myself. "That was unexpected. Do better."

20 days in April and all of May, June, and July: all to finish one book, a book that was partially written to start with. A book that was over 100,000 words. Four months, but only three days a week, so that's about 50 total days. More than 2,000 words per session, though. Each session packed with struggles over character voices, with the abrupt arrival of subprimary characters who clamored for their own scenes and individual voices, and four different plots instead of the two I had anticipated. A whole month lost to *Web*.

I was happy with the book. One blessing in the whole four month struggle.

Specific goals would have helped – Lesson 23. Weekly word counts would have helped. Anticipating how many words would need to be written each week and each day would have helped.

At the start, I should have estimated the total number of words, figured out a do-able words per session, and divided. Instead, I just started writing. After all, that's what I've done from the very beginning. I work through the Foundations and the Visioning and the Analysis stages, then I write and write and write and write and write until I reach the end.

After *Web* went up, I decided to take a few days off. I piddled. I caught up on my blogs, all the way to Christmas!

On Labor Day weekend, I got the news that my house had sold. It had only been on the market since late June. Great news, for it sold within 90 days. Bad news, for I had to be out in less than two weeks.

My furniture for a 3 BR house wouldn't fit into the studio. I rented one storage unit, realized that wasn't enough, and rented another. I made plans for a larger place. I do like to nest with all my things around me. I thought, *This won't take long.* Stupid me.

I haven't even talked about my nephew's wedding on September 30. I mean, over the summer I wasn't really involved in the planning or anything. It was a little stressful. I won't go into those stresses. I mean, do they really matter? Sigh.

I lost all of September.

I gutted plans for a nonfiction book (and still haven't returned to those plans).

I gutted the book that would be the next direction for my Edie Roones pseudonym (and still haven't returned to those plans either).

Lesson 24 = Take out what won't fit. Don't lose it; hold on to it. I will get to these books soon.

I updated the next Enclave book, *Dream a Deadly Dream*, a book I truly loved when I wrote it, fell in love with all over again when I refreshed it with the new *Web* insertions to the Alstera storyline, and published it.

I turned to the next book in my goals list, the next Into Death, book 2 in a planned 3-book series. And struggled again.

Consider 2017. Changing jobs. Moving over 100 miles away. Radically downsizing. Knowing my home wasn't permanent. Coping with distractions from people I love. Coping with new members of the family.

I wasn't going to achieve 9 books. And it looked like I wouldn't hit 7, either.

Six serious issues. I thought I was handling them well.

I wasn't. Silly me.

Because I hadn't properly planned my writing for the year.

Look what I was trying to do. In addition to the 6 Life Rolls, I was trying to write more words than I had ever written in a year.

- 150,000 words on the first three novels of the year
- 32,000 on the nonfiction book
- 200,000 on the first two Remi Black books
- 50,000 on the seventh book.

That's a doable 1,200 words per day *every* day of the year. I wasn't writing *every* day. I wasn't even writing five days a week. Try three days a week. That's 432,000 divided by 52 weeks = 8,308 words per week. Divide that total by 3 to get the three-day per session writing for 2,769.

And I thought 1,500 words per session would be sufficient.

I was an idiot.

Writers are word merchants, but we need to do math quite a bit. I hate math, but I'm doing it now, believe me. Lesson 25.

Did I achieve my goal? Come back tomorrow and find out.

APRIL 7 ~ WIN-LOSE-WIN

Current Project :: *To Wield the Wind*
Project Stage :: Sketching Ideas
Today's Word Count: 0,000
Total Word Count: 10,144 / 33,000
Goal: 5,000 words per week
Weekly Words Achieved 4,424
Project Dates: March 25 to May 5 Publication

Thursday I had commitments start up. Company came. I lost sleep, but I didn't lose any writing time. Win-lose-win.

Friday I volunteered at the reception desk at my church, one tiny thing that I can do. Came home to the surprise of company still here. Had to dog-sit, which is helpful because it forces me to move more than I would. Had to cook unexpectedly. Win-Lose-Win-Lose.

Saturday, got tugged into the Spring-sprung yard. Raking. Spreading dirt. More raking. Lopping branches and weeds and roots. More raking. Carrying to street for the brush pickup. Fixing a quick and reviving lunch. More carrying. More raking. More lopping. More and more. Cooking after clean-up. Laundry. Thank God for baseball. Lose-lose-lose-lose. . . . The exercise is the only win.

Today is Sunday. I'm sunburned. I'm weary. I'm doing this blog. I need to write 600-plus words. I will, before I post this so I can get the totals correct. Lose-lose-lose-win.

Monday, I must pay bills, a monthly requirement that I absolutely hate but which keeps me on track. Lose-win.

Commitments to family and friends and those ugly obligations are necessary, especially for writers. They keep us engaged in the world and with the world. Lesson 26.

We writers want to live in our heads. We want nothing except time to write. When intrusions intrude, we go mentally kicking and screaming while we put on fake smiles--and rarely real ones.

These are three long blog posts in a row. Next week I'm buckling down to writing. I want to get more than my 5,000 words before this Friday. The week after, I still need to finish promos for May, get my word count in, and stay alert and ready for church celebrations around Easter.

I'm anticipating the next two weeks. That's an important lesson, remember?

- Wednesday night is choir practice, the next-to-last preparation for four upcoming worship services of the most important week in all Christendom.

- Next weekend will be someone's birthday! I will cook on Friday (the cake, the rolls), and on Saturday I'll cook more and eat and talk and laugh and walk the dog.

- Sunday is Palm Sunday, an important celebration at my church. Our last choir practice on Wednesday is followed by Maundy Thursday, Good Friday, and then Easter.

I remember when I didn't properly anticipate. Remembering those failures now helps me plan every week.

Back in 2017 I planned to publish nine books, remember?

- I had a three-book combo to publish in the first third of the year. I started them in 2016; I just had to finish them.

- In May I published a nonfiction book, one that I had tinkered with for years. No problem.

- I did struggle through the summer with the jumbled-up manuscript that would be my first Remi Black. *Weave a Wizardry Web*, the MS mess that was my focus in yesterday's blog, eventually resolved itself into a really great story.

- The second Remi Black flowed like mercury. Refreshing *Dream a Deadly Dream* gave me joy. I didn't really have to touch the book, just bring it into line with the changes that occurred to the Enclave and the Alstera storyline during *Web*. With *Dream*, I thought I was back on track.

- Because of the summer struggles, I gutted two of the planned books then slaved to get the last book published.

- The 7th book would be shorter, a little bit more than a novella. This would be the next Into Death book, which is my M.A. Lee pseudonym, and I wanted it to be available as a Christmas sale. I planned to put it out by the end of November, plenty of time for holiday buyers.

Not easy peasy.

The life rolls hurt. I didn't realize how much the disruptions to my habitual writing schedule would hurt. I had to develop—slowly—new writing habits, which including working around noise! We can write anywhere. We don't want to, but we can. Lesson 27.

I thought I had sense by removing two books from the goals list. But I didn't have sense. I would have only the last couple of days of October and all of November to write the upcoming novella. Barely 35 days.

I was proud of myself for achieving six novels. I hadn't missed a single blog or promo post. Surely I could finish a 7th book.

I launched into the story.

Christmas with Death flew. I managed to publish it on November 28. But I had many stressful days of writing. I lost the joy of writing. I allowed myself to be tugged in multiple directions when I should have been writing.

Still, if I was going to meet my plans for 2018, I needed to keep cracking. I was going to try for 9 books again.

With the January book, *The Key to Secrets*, I had a lot of fun with ballads and the old crazy lady who sang them, Constable Hector Evans and his true love, and the mysterious murders he had to solve in a handful of days. The tagline for the book was perfect: Debutantes should snare fiancés, not murder them.

The joy of writing was back.

I have planned novels and nonfiction in detail since 2015. With Foundations and Visioning and Analysis completed early in 2017, I expected no problems. I drafted *The Key to Secrets* entirely on computer. After all, I had spent years upon years drafting work product entirely on computer with the barest list of inked ideas to guide me.

I forgot that there is a vast difference between creative flow and critical flow.

I forgot that there is a vast difference between nonfiction writing and fiction writing.

I forgot that each book is vastly different from all others.

Silly me. I still had three important lessons to learn.

Those lessons are for tomorrow. I have bills to pay, remember? Can't go to the 10th of the month without paying them.

So, writing tonight. Bills tomorrow and no anticipated words, then buckling down.

APRIL 8 ~ CRITICAL VS. CREATIVE

Current Project :: *To Wield the Wind*
Project Stage :: Sketching Ideas
Today's Word Count: 0,000
Total Word Count: 10,144 / 33,000
Goal: 5,000 words per week
Weekly Words Achieved 0,000
Project Dates: March 25 to May 5 Publication

I'm finishing the blog from Sunday about lessons I needed to learn: critical vs. creative, writing nonfiction vs. fiction, and books that are vastly different.

I had bills to pay today. No words written. Tomorrow I start pushing for 5,000 words this week. I don't anticipate a word-filled weekend.

I published *The Key to Secrets* on schedule in mid-January. The hardest part of that book was keeping track of the murder clues. Checked the box for the first M.A. Lee.

Next up would be my second book for 2018, an Edie Roones. I would be refreshing an old manuscript. Easy peasy? Nope. Trouble reared its ugly head again. The Edie Roones wouldn't come together.

When things don't work out, turn to the next book. Lesson 28. I thought that was the only lesson that I needed to learn. Wrong.

I switched to the third book in the plan, the next Remi Black, another refresh of an old manuscript. Easy peasy. I had a printed-out manuscript and wrote the revisions and corrections there, then transferred them to computer. *Sing a Graveyard Song* flew toward publication.

Didn't learn the right lesson, though.

I returned to the Edie Roones. And stumbled again. The old manuscript wouldn't come together. Something was drastically wrong with it. I trashed what I had on computer and worked out new scenes with pen and paper. Started a third time. Got fifty pages in and stumbled again. Back to the handwriting. Another 30 pages or so. At least the story was moving along. On paper *Winter Sorcery* took unexpected turns, morphing into a richer, deeper story. It was also running shorter than the other Edie Roones books, but every time I added in details, it felt artificially padded, so those came back out.

Between a mix of handwriting and typing, I finished *Winter Sorcery* and published the day before the Spring Equinox, barely in winter.

Here's what I should have learned with both of these books. The creative ideas happen (for me) with pen and paper. On computer, I don't let the words flow on and on. I back up and correct. That's critical brain controlling creative brain.

When I'm on paper, I just let the words flow out. I'm a fast typist, but I'm faster writing by hand. The words can pour, like a river in flood.

Some people use dictation software for their creative flow, then they return and correct. This separates the creative from the critical. Lesson 29.

Next on the list was the next M.A. Lee, *The Key for Spies*. I started up on computer and fell into the same problems as before. When the struggling happened, I decided to work on *Think like a Pro*, updating and revising. I switched back and forth between the two books. I couldn't figure out why the nonfiction book poured out on the computer but the fiction book wouldn't.

Still slogging through *K4Spies*—I hadn't even reached 100 good pages, I finished the nonfiction book, decided to do *Think / Pro: A Planner for Writers*. Dealt with layout issues. Finished it. Decided to do *2 * 0 * 4 Lifestyle*, another planner, and still struggled with *K4Spies*. Into October.

I was seriously behind my goals. Three nonfiction books and still under 100 pages for *K4Spies*.

I belatedly comprehended—for I already knew—nonfiction is critical brain that is easier than the creative brain needed for fiction. Lesson 30. The only creative part of nonfiction is the planning and the sentence craft parts.

For *K4Spies*, I decided to gut what I had. I started on a day when the internet was down, my laptop was acting up, and had to work with pen and paper.

25 great pages.

On the next day I transferred them to the computer and tried to write more. Nope. Nothing doing.

The next day was a long drive. Four hours in the backseat of a car. I took a notebook. Wound up with close to 50 great pages.

I didn't touch the laptop again until I had the book in a completed rough shape. New characters had entered the story. New action scenes wrote themselves while I watched in amazement. The book hit the mark of 98,000 words when I finally transferred it to computer. All the while, distractions occurred, commitments and obligations tugged me away from writing. Yet the novel poured out every time I managed to sit down with pen and paper.

I learned that nonfiction is logical and thus critical brain, more suited to my computer-based writing. Fiction, for me, needs the permission to scribble, zoom, scratch out, re-start, and rush like a torrent. You know, messy creativity.

The next book, *The Key with Hearts*, was written and finished in 35 days.

I'm sticking with pen and paper for creative fiction. I learned my lesson ~ 30.

It just took me a couple of years.

I know. I'm not the brightest bulb in the socket.

APRIL 9 ~ EAT THE FROG FIRST

Current Project :: *To Wield the Wind*
Project Stage :: Rough Shape
Today's Word Count: 1,804
Total Word Count: 11,684 / 33,000
Goal: 5,000 words per week
Weekly Words Achieved 1,804
Project Dates: March 25 to May 5 Publication

We've covered thirty lessons over the last 8 days.

The last four blogs, especially, have turned into a "Me, me, me!". It's difficult to write about a writer's month without talking about my life.

So what has today been?

First, I ate a frog. That's a bit of writer's advice that I picked up at a writer's conference last summer's end. "Eat the frog first thing in the morning." Do the task that you most don't want to do first ~ Lesson 31.

Today, my first thing was the volunteer writing that I do for my choir. A choir member or musician answers questions. I take their answers and rework them to sound like an interview. It's a bit like ghostwriting. It's hard because I want everyone to sound wonderful, and it's doubly hard because it needs to be presented perfectly: no errors!

Then we planned meals for the week and headed off on our errands, the last at the grocery store.

After lunch, I got interested in listening to the Miss Julia book that my niece is reading aloud. I believe it's the first Miss Julia, by Ann B. Ross, and it's hilarious. I started off by only half-listening, since I was doing some writerly research, then I became interested in the story.

I had to abandon that fun read in order to achieve my necessary word count for the day.

Today's writing session started with a review of Sunday's jot list. I began by re-writing it, transferring to another sheet the ideas that I knew I wouldn't get to. Next came planning by a quick jot list for the details that needed to happen in the next scene. Then I started that scene by grounding with descriptive sentences that gradually led straight into an action sequence.

This was a good day, with 1,804 words, nearly twice what I had planned. The intuitive muse popped out details that I didn't plan for: always good.

I actually ended today's session twice. The first time I had over 1,200 words. I was going to create a jot list. I even pulled out the paper for the note and wrote the first two items—only to realize that I had a lot of little details that I might forget. So I wrote the next 600 words. The muse gave me more interesting details as well as a hint of backstory, totally unanticipated. The creativity is flowing now.

When I reached a good stopping point, I created my jot list for tomorrow. I reviewed what I had transferred over at the beginning of today and added more.

Today's 1,804 words finished out a scene and transitioned into its sequel. Dwight V. Swain explains scenes and sequels in his *Techniques of the Best Selling Writer*, a book that I urge every writing newbie and gonnabie to have on their bookshelves.

"Eating the Frog" first allowed the creative muse to work while I took care of my errands and other ticky things for the day. Instead of the dreaded work hanging over me and gradually depressing the muse, the ghostwriting ghosted away. When I put bum in chair for *To Wield the Wind*, I was eager to start.

The weekly goal of 5,000 words now has 1804 banked = leaving 3,196 to go for this week. Of the entire story, 38.5 % is now in rough shape. The story is creating the foundation for its climax as well as building a continuing conflict for the next books. The fantasy of the story is becoming more fantastical. The two primaries are becoming more sympathetic. And the antagonists are becoming more in number as well as trickier to defeat.

That's it for me today. I'll crowd in a little reading before turning out the light on the day.

April 10 ~ The Tax Man Cometh

Current Project :: *To Wield the Wind*
Project Stage :: Rough Shape
Today's Word Count: 1,760
Total Word Count: 15,248 / 33,000
Goal: 5,000 words per week
Weekly Words Achieved 3,364
Project Dates: March 25 to May 5 Publication

Have you paid your taxes for the year?

Did you take all your deductions for writing?

Have you recorded your sales / profits? Your expenses / losses?

If you're renting or paying a mortgage, the size of your writing space can be deducted. As long as your space is solely devoted to writing, then it is countable.

Don't forget your deductions for the cost of doing business. These expenses include printer ink/paper, flash drives or portable hard drives, cloud subscriptions, binders or storage for manuscript hard copies, sticky notes/flags, highlighters, pens, scissors, tape . . . . If you use these legitimately and solely for your business, you can count them.

A surprise deduction for me was my mileage, especially those trips I use for interviews or research or inspiration.

The cell phone was not a surprise deduction. I depend upon it to connect with my cover designer and for research and more.

Cover designers and printing costs as well as advertising and marketing are all legitimate business expenses.

For taxes, you need to fill out Schedule C, which is for expenses incurred in businesses. Schedule C includes~

8] Advertising

10] Commissions and fees

11] Contract labor

15] Insurance related to your business. This is not health or life insurance.

17] Legal and professional services. This pays for your CPA who does your taxes for you.

18] Office expenses

20] Rent or lease of vehicles for business

22] Supplies. See, this is that list above.

23] Taxes and licenses.

24] Travel and meals. (This is the exciting one.)

25] Utilities. Yes, indeedy, your electricity and water and gas bills can be partially deducted, based on the size of your office space.

You can also add other expenses, such as cover designer costs (which might fit under Contract Labor, but my CPAs have always counted it separately) and conferences and workshops and reference materials.

When you have books printed and hold them in stock for sale at conferences and the like, you have *inventory*. You will need to record the dollar amount for the beginning vs. the ending of the year. Any materials, supplies, and other costs related to that inventory are also deductible.

As you work on last year's taxes, consider your accumulating deductions for this year. Create a budget book. In my first years, I ran single-entry bookkeeping, with the out-go and in-come as a single column. This year, I'm considering double-entry, separating costs (out-go) from earnings (in-come. Geez, when that word is hyphenated, it takes on a completely new meaning.)

Track all of the above possible expenses and earnings throughout this year. Your life will be easier at the next tax time.

Keep your returns and all tax-related materials (in case of an audit) for seven years. A fire safe is a smart investment—as well as a business expense.

In 2017, the year I changed my jobs and moved—two major life events—I definitely needed a CPA. Anyone experiencing a major life event—including marriage and death and babies—needs a CPA to do the taxes for that year. The first year that you file as a writer, you need to use a CPA just to learn how to do it. Find one that you can trust and move forward.

For years, I hired a CPA for my tax preparation. I know that I spent much more than I should have, but the sense of security and lack of stress related to tax season was worth that money to me. I don't regret paying my CPAs, especially the one that I used last year, the year of the two major life events. The lady found many more deductions than I would have, AND those deductions basically paid her fee. But her fee was elevated because I had so many deductions which meant so many forms to fill out.

This year, I did my own tax preparation. I may have missed a few deductions. Oh well.

The famous online tax service that I used walked me through the process. It was low-stress, easy to understand, and at a cost that wasn't three times what I expected. I used my returns from previous years to guide my gathering of materials and numbers.

So today's Lesson 32 is tax-related: make sure you gather up your expenses and earnings, take as many deductions as you can, use a CPA for your first time filing as a writer—to learn how to do it, and as this year advances, keep tax time constantly in mind. 4 major lessons.

APRIL 11 ~ COCOONS

Current Project :: *To Wield the Wind*
Project Stage :: Sketching Ideas
Today's Word Count: 1,430
Total Word Count: 16,678 / 33,000
Goal: 5,000 words per week
Weekly Words Achieved 4,994
Project Dates: March 25 to May 5 Publication

I had trouble starting today. The jot list wasn't the problem. The starting sentences were. They didn't flow. I backed out, re-wrote them, then decided to let the story steep for a while. I did a lot of little chores, some related to life, some related to writing. Life stepped in and distracted me for most of the afternoon.

Yet because I started the day by reading and re-working my jot list, the muse twirled things around while I dealt with little chores that needed to be done and would have to be, either today or tomorrow. Better to do them today.

When I finally broke free of life and sat down at my desk, the time read 4:30. I started a new jot list then opened up my notebook. And the sentences flowed out, like the swiftly running creek the characters are camping beside.

I took a break for supper then came back and finished up.

Some days we writers wake up with the starting sentences in our heads. We can't wait to sit down and write. On other days, we have an idea of our start but not the specific sentences. Those come, however, as soon as we are ready for the first words. Other days, like today, we need a bit more contemplation.

One key to success, the key I am currently using—and methods will evolve and transform, remember—is the daily word count. It's a reasonable word count. When the blue sky and warm weather is calling, something has to draw us back to our writing.

I did contemplate sitting on my deck and writing—but the pollen is turning the table and chair and my car and the pavement the crayon color of Green Yellow.

You've seen that color, right? In the box it's this pretty light green of a rich hue. When you start coloring with it, it's this pale yellow with a hint of green. You can't hardly see it.

I just looked at the Wiki page of Crayola colors. That Green Yellow is no longer classified by that name. The powers of Crayola are calling it "inchworm" now.

I wonder if the "inchworm" crayon has the same transformative value as the original Green Yellow. I wonder if the "inchworm" color is like the inchworm itself.

Writers can be inchworms.

Writers are writing even when they're not writing ~ Lesson 33. Our ideas are inching along, just like the inchworm, waiting for the cocoon, waiting for the transformation to be complete. Then the words will emerge, beautiful as a butterfly.

APRIL 12 ~ SIX WORDS SHORT

Current Project :: *To Wield the Wind*
Project Stage :: Sketching Ideas
Today's Word Count: 0,000
Total Word Count: 16,678 / 33,000
Goal: 5,000 words per week
Weekly Words Achieved 4,994
Project Dates: March 25 to May 5 Publication

Today is Friday. On Thursday, I reached a total of 4,994 words for the week—six words from the weekly goal of 5,000 on my current primary project *To Wield the Wind*. I did write today, just not on *WieldWind*.

If you haven't read yesterday's blog, I'll wait while you do so. Go on. ☺.

Some people would have gone back and written those six words, just to have the goal completed for the week.

If I counted my jot list, I would definitely have those six words. But I'm not counting my jot list.

Are these your questions?

Q1 ~ Why didn't she write those six words?

Q2 ~ What will she do now that she's reached this week's goal with days remaining?

Q3 ~ Is she done writing for the week?

Did you consider these answers?

A1 ~ Why didn't I write those six words? Well, I didn't know I needed to. I did the math for my daily word count after I put the writing away. I had finished the evening's blog by then. I was shutting every down for the night.

Which meant my writing brain was already shut down.

Can you answer this question: *Should I go back and add those six little words just so I can say done?* Or answer this one: *"Is a writer's writing ever done?"*

Nope and nope.

Think about adding words. *Isn't that the critical editor trying to go in and fix the manuscript while the creative muse has charge of it?* What will the editor's injection into creativity *do* to the muse?

A2 ~ If I had those six words written, what will I do with my writing for the week? After all, I've achieved the week's goal.

Does a runner stop moving? Does a composer stop writing music when the symphony's done?

Nope and nope.

Goal achieved. I can turn to something else with a clear conscience. Between now and Sunday evening, I know the right time for writing will come. Now I can work on a non-writing project without worrying about completing the goal. Or I can write more. Or I can dip into the next project. Or do all three. Or nothing at all.

That's the joy of achieving the weekly goal. It's not a burden. It's do-able.

A3 ~ Am I done for the week? Certainly not.

Even if I'm not actively writing, I'll still mull over the next scenes. I may sketch out ideas. I may work on the rough shape.

Or not.

I pushed Tuesday, Wednesday, and Thursday because I had commitments for today and tomorrow. I knew that I would likely not be able to write on these two days.

We have a big birthday celebration for a family member mid-day Saturday. Cooking before. Clean-up afterward. I might have a little time Saturday evening, after everyone's gone their merry ways, and I finally have some solitude.

We never know exactly what's coming—here's Lesson 34. I know what's planned (a previous lesson, btw). Other things may interfere—and will.

Knowing where I am with the goal and knowing how little needs to be accomplished, I can leave my writing space and enter life. Cheerfully. Without guilt. Able to be in the present. Keeping the joy of writing.

That's the point.

Coming up, I need to talk about connecting with my cover designer. Once again, my cover designer has delivered something so completely better than my vision that I'm overwhelmed. The cover art for *To Wield the Wind* is currently gracing the header for the Remi Black website. Ain't it great?

APRIL 13 ~ WONDERS NEVER CEASE

Current Project :: *To Wield the Wind*
Project Stage :: Rough Shape
Today's Word Count: 550
Total Word Count: 17,228 / 33,000
Goal: 5,000 words per week
Weekly Words Achieved 5,544
Project Dates: March 25 to May 5 Publication

Wonders never cease.

I didn't expect to write anything on my current project today. We had a big celebration, all sorts of prep, time to be in the present with the people I love, chatting and laughing. Then clean up.

But being ready for opportunities for writing is part of being a writer.

Got a call about 1 ½ hours before time to start cooking, delaying the celebration. That delay gave me time to sneak off to my writing space and tear out some words.

No, literally, tear out words. I trashed over two pages, 440 words. Then I wrote 990, which puts me 550 on the goal.

544 words more than the six I needed at the end of writing on Thursday.

I also know what I'll be writing in the next scene. My jot list turned into a loose sketch.

I spent the morning—before I knew about the delay—mulling murder. My next project will be a Regency murder mystery under my M.A. Lee pseudonym. When I figure out the reason and the method for the murder, I can construct the basic foundation.

And this blog document is reaching over 11,900 words, which averages 915 words per day since April 1, the "No Fooling" blog that began this *Write a Book in a Month*.

So, here I am, not expecting to work on writing, and I've been into three projects this day alone.

Because I was ready for any opportunity. Because I looked for the opportunity.

Readiness and Awareness, Lesson 35 for today.

And tomorrow is still to come.

APRIL 14 ~ ONE PROJECT, TWO PROJECT

Current Project :: *To Wield the Wind*
Project Stage :: Sketching Ideas
Today's Word Count: 0,000
Total Word Count: 17,228 / 33,000
Goal: 5,000 words per week
Weekly Words Achieved 5,544
Project Dates: March 25 to May 5 Publication

I can't write two fiction projects at the same time. I've tried. I've tried alternating days, halving the week three days and three, and writing on one project until I'm drained then switching to the other, flipping back and forth.

Those methods merely slow down my creative muse, as if I'm confusing her.

I likely confused her today.

I can write fiction and nonfiction and blogs simultaneously. I can do the rough/draft on one project while I edit/correct a second fiction project. These work processes use the creative and critical brains, easy enough to keep muse away from editor.

And I know that I need to take certain breaks from creative outpouring. Otherwise, I run ahead of the muse and run out of ideas and words. Slow-downs are necessary, therefore.

Knowing this, I schedule one day of every week for pure critical work. Sometimes I will add more critical work. I also try to schedule pure creativity one day of every week.

April 1st was a pure creativity day. I sketched ideas.

Today, April 15, was another pure creativity day.

I mentioned yesterday that I had mulled over murder throughout the morning until I could seize the opportunity to pour out some writing for my current project.

The murder is my next project, book 10 in the Hearts in Hazard Regency mystery series, under my pseudonym M.A. Lee.

I did a little mulling on Friday, but I wasn't happy with anything that I worked out.

Yesterday, when I realized that I had achieved my week's word-count goal, I decided to use today as a pure creativity exercise. Last thing for last evening was looking over the ideas that I had generated on Friday and realizing those ideas just wouldn't work. I needed another direction. Since the title—*The Hazard of Secrets*—wasn't generating ideas on its own, I wrote a quick note to try a different direction. "Start with names," I wrote.

After today settled down, I fetched a clipboard and the ideas that I had, then stared into space. Lesson 36: Ideas come out of blankness. Don't fear the blankness.

The first name that popped up was one that I didn't really like. I came up with many more, writing them on paper like a high school girl trying out variations of her name matched to her boyfriend's. None of the names fit, not really. I returned to the first name, twisted it a little, and suddenly I could see the character hiding in shadows. Never settle. You know you've found the right name (or idea or motif or title) when a scene develops.

Story comes out of many things. An image, a name, a title, a motif, blankness ~ all of these will generate events. It's the writer who will shape the events into the story.

I started writing: Clarey hiding in the shadows, fingers pressed to her mouth to keep from making any sound.

When I finished, I had 1300 words—an opening scene, the secrets that both dual protagonists were hiding, and the murder that would occur.

I won't touch this project in the foreseeable future. My focus remains *To Wield the Wind*, which is still going strongly. Lesson 37: Waiting won't kill the story. Stay focused until the primary project is nearing completion. The waiting will improve the next project—and may spark ideas for the current project.

To prevent Muse-confusion, I will work tomorrow on promotions for May. Yep, I work a few weeks in advance. I'm actually behind. Taxes then bill-paying kept me from working on the May posts as soon as I would normally have. Yet everything falls into place: I need something to break the different creative projects. Promotions will do that.

No words anticipated tomorrow—but who knows? As happened on Saturday, it pays to be ready.

Coming up I *will* talk about finding a cover designer. Covers are extremely important. They are the first lures to attract a reader to your book.

April 15 ~ Promotions

Current Project :: *To Wield the Wind*
Project Stage :: Sketching Ideas
Today's Word Count: 0,000
Total Word Count: 17,228 / 33,000
Goal: 5,000 words per week
Weekly Words Achieved 5,544
Percent of Project Completed :: 52%
Project Dates: March 25 to May 5 Publication

Well, it's certainly a good thing that I didn't plan to write creatively today. The local utilities were working on the street just outside my window. The motors, the sounds like rattling chains, the vibration from whatever the workers were doing to the ground, all were extremely distracting.

Today I worked on the promo posts for May. This means blogs for the two websites (one for fiction, the other for non-fiction), the posts on social media, and blog posts for each of my pseudonyms. Before Christmas, I realized that Promo Day was taking two days, not one, so I counted the number of posts. 64! That's too many. And that wasn't counting ads for Christmas selling.

Granted, that was before Christmas, when people are searching for gifts, but 64 is too many.

Since then, I've tried to knock that number in half.

This month, since I'm trying to post every day for Remi Black, the number will increase—although I will use some of the RB posts as links for social media.

So here we go.

1st: Look at the calendar to see if any book anniversaries will occur; schedule their celebration on the website blog and on social media.

2nd: I am slowly writing (under my M.A. Lee pseudonym) a book about punctuation, more of an explanation on the ins and outs of punx rather than exercises, which are easy to find while the explanations are woefully inadequate. The book is geared for the high school market which needs secondary level information.

Much of the online educational material is too simple for students aiming for an academic college or university; the explanations in current textbooks provide bare-bones information. With grammar and composition, details are necessary to handle the intricacies and exceptions that always occur. For people who only want to prepare students for elementary achievement, the online information—unless it's geared for the advanced placement courses—lacks the necessary complexity.

Higher levels of learning require complex knowledge, not simplistic.

Currently, I am finishing a set of blogs on the colon and moving to the semicolon before tackling the comma. Those blogs go up on the website today after which comes a link to a social media post with a catchy tagline to snare attention. These blogs and linked posts connected as Monster Monday. Eventually, I'll start putting out lesson plans for the Home School market

3rd: My publishing imprint is Writers Ink Books. W.Ink Wednesday on social media on the Writers Ink page offers a link to the current focus. Book anniversaries, free chapters, glimpses of story development, cover releases, and recommended books that I am reading all fall under this. W.Ink Wednesday is linked to the social media posts on that day as well as some Snippet Saturdays.

4th: Each of my pseudonyms has its own Blogspot and social media presence. The appropriate W.Ink Wednesday posts also show up here. I try to have two posts a month for each writing entity.

5th: Snippet Saturday started as a way to connect via social media for a third time during the week, but they have evolved into important quotations. Last fall several quotations from Anne Morrow Lindbergh's *A Gift from the Sea* were showcased, and my reaction to those quotations and the book itself became a blog. At the start of the year the snippets were inspired by Marie Kondo's *Life-Changing Magic of Tidying Up*. Snippets do bounce around in focus.

Do I think all of these posts are helpful in spreading the word of my books? I would hope so, but I suspect the Snippet Saturday is having little or no effect on increasing audience.

Monster Monday helps me slowly write that punx book. Other blogs served as background material for my nonfiction writers' guides *Think like a Pro* and *Old Geeky Greeks*. Several writers have asked for advice; I try to be helpful.

W.Ink Wednesday on social media and on the website blogs is the only purely promotional/marketing posts that I do.

I've run ads in the past. Before Christmas, I sought out advertising opportunities for my books. I believe my sales increased because of the ads.

It's difficult to say what has the greatest effect on driving sales of my books.

Except that the number one guarantee of selling more books is to be a great story-teller.

And the number two guarantee of selling more books is to write more books.

Promotional posts are a long day of work for me. I burn out quickly and take breaks constantly—probably as often as I should. When I'm writing and the words are flowing, I don't like to take breaks.

When I finally settle into my nest, I will likely write in the morning and try to handle all the business in the afternoon.

For now, one day in each work week seems to be working until I have a new release. Then I use an extra day for those posts and another day to create a video trailer. I do love video trailers. They're the one promotional post that I really enjoy creating.

Here's a link to my latest trailer: https://www.youtube.com/watch?v=JyDlvYQf8ow

So, my posts for the month of May are now completed except for the slots I left open to promote *To Wield the Wind*—which I do expect to publish in early May!

Oh! What's today's lesson? 38 ~ Promotional posts.

April 16 ~ Covers

Current Project :: *To Wield the Wind*
Project Stage :: Rough Shape
Today's Word Count: 1,800
Total Word Count: 19,098 / 33,000
Goal: 5,000 words per week
Weekly Words Achieved 1,800
Project Dates: March 25 to May 5 Publication

One of the greatest expenses that an indie writer will have is the cost of a professional cover ~ Lesson 39.

Yes, yes, people say the editorial cost is the highest one. Developmental editors and content editors and line editors are expensive.

Let me argue with that. First of all, you need to trust your instincts about your story, immerse yourself in story development, and not depend on developmental editors. You need to build your own writing chops and not depend on someone else to do it.

Lesson 40 ~ Be familiar with your own story. Devote the necessary time to catch the plot holes and character discrepancies and setting glitches. Finally, line editors are a fancy term for a copyreader. Don't pay a fancy price for a job any high school English teacher can do well.

Not everyone has the best grammar. Even people with great grammar knowledge are never right 100% of the time, so I would invest in a copyreader. However, you can hire a local English teacher for much less than the cost of a line editor.

Now that's out of the way.

But what about ISBNs and the copyright registration fee? Those are expensive. Well, yes, the upfront cost for 10 ISBNs can make you wince, but 10 is a bargain over just one. If you handle your copyright registration fee each time you publish, then the cost is not gigantic. These are two of those necessary expenses classified as the "Cost of Doing Business" ~ Lesson 41.

Your book covers are a different matter. Cover designers are skilled graphic artists who understand the importance of the aesthetic, that subtle and almost indefinable something that sets one cover off from another one and draws readers to the book.

The cover is the first selling point for your book. Don't turn people away at this point. Charm them.

When I first aimed toward publication, back in 2015, I was naïve enough to think formatting the book would be the hard part and finding a cover designer would be easy. I should have flipped that. It took me 18 months to find a cover designer who understood the aesthetic that I desired and was able to deliver it.

I did countless searches using different search inquiries on different search engines, all which bring up different results. Google and Bing and Yahoo and DuckDuckGo and others. I used all sorts of keywords.

I finally found my cover designers by scanning for covers that I liked in the online market distributors, Amazon and Smashwords and iBooks. The book's sample pages took me far enough in to get an acknowledgement for the cover designer, and that's how I found mine.

Cover designers should be professionals with an artistic aesthetic that coincides with your vision for your books and your author brand. They should stay abreast of the field in directions for covers and ahead of the field in techniques and methods.

I've been with that company since 2015 and have no plans to leave them. They're becoming more and more successful, which means they can demand higher prices and booking covers can get a little antsy. We've had glitches, caused on my end from not understanding the design process. On both ends we strive for chatty amiability, but we've never met and probably never will.

Unless I win the mega-million-dollar lottery. Then I'll fly over to meet them and reward them appropriately and individually for the wonderful work that they do.

We connect via email. They send images as drafts then final, using various methods depending on the file sizes. As soon as I approve a draft, they invoice me through PayPal, and I pay promptly.

Over the years they've had a few changes to their contract terms, and I can spin scenarios about writers who must have caused those changes.

And here's another reason to keep your hard-earned money going to professional cover designers—you don't have to deal with s**t. There's a lot of whiney NON-professionals out there. People who claim they'll do one thing but don't. People who don't proofread their covers and send it back with titles misspelled. People who claim to be abreast of the field but only churn out covers that look like last year's bestseller—which means they're *two years* behind. People who say they'll be finished on a particular date but miss it by weeks.

Don't give these people any money. Depend on professionalism.

And be professional yourself.

Your best behavior is to put yourself in another person's shoes before you start making demands.

That's a life skill, by the way.

Think I'm blowing smoke about NON-professionals? Try this blog, which came across a writer's forum to which I belong early this morning entitled "Professionals Don't Act Like This" on theauthorlife.com :: https://theauthorlife.com/professionals-dont-act-like-this/

APRIL 17 ~ FRITTERY JITTERY

Current Project :: *To Wield the Wind*
Project Stage :: Rough Shape
Today's Word Count: 1,125
Total Word Count: 20,223/ 33,000
Goal: 5,000 words per week
Weekly Words Achieved 2,925
Project Dates: March 25 to May 5 Publication

Today's one of those frittery days when it's difficult to concentrate on the writing and it's impossible to pin down the reason so we can knock it totally away.

So I threw in some laundry.

And still couldn't settle to writing. I mean, I know I *have* to write today. I need a day like yesterday. Yesterday I almost reached double my needed word count. Yesterday was a wonderful day.

Today, I struggled to write a half-page after a couple of hours. Only 110 words. Sigh.

So I re-arranged my work space. Total re-arrangement. Set up a different desktop. Shifted the printer over and away. Moved the two-drawer filing cabinet across the room, beside the bookcase. Unplugged and plugged in all the necessary wires.

Got another three-quarters of a page. Only 165. 275 for the day. Sigh.

Went to choir practice. A looooonnnngggg practice, for we had Maundy Thursday and Good Friday and Easter to prepare for.

Came back. With very little time to write, wrote three and three-quarters pages. Total word count at 1,125. 850 words in less than an hour. After struggling the whole day.

Sigh.

Granted, today's scene was a difficult one. Tomorrow should be easier. Got the difficult conversation between the dual primaries completed. Well, half-completed. They can't have the other part of the difficult conversation until after the Ordeal scene.

But we're moving.

And that's Lesson 42. Keep moving on. Write the scenes that are hard as you reach them. Otherwise, when you reach the end of your rough draft, you have all horribly hard scenes ahead of you.

No wonder so many newbies and wannabies never finish manuscript, if they procrastinate about the hard scenes and never get to writing them.

Here's Part Two of today's lesson. Keep trying for that daily word count, even if you have to come back to it numerous times. Even if your brain doesn't want to settle to writing because the scene will be horribly hard.

Keep moving. Keep trying. Get there.

When the evening draws to a close, don't spend excess time on a blog. Get some sleep.

APRIL 18 ~ FLIPPING OUT

Current Project :: *To Wield the Wind*
Project Stage :: Rough Shape
Today's Word Count: 0,000
Total Word Count: 20,223 / 33,000
Goal: 5,000 words per week
Weekly Words Achieved 2,925
Project Dates: March 25 to May 5 Publication

So, this is a busy week, which I knew going in. In addition to regular commitments, I have more commitments for Thursday and Friday and an all-day event on Saturday that I knew about but had forgotten until I was reminded by a kind person on Tuesday. Yikes!

That reminder may have contributed to yesterday's frittery jittery.

In passing, as part of an earlier section, I mentioned that planning for the week is essential to the writer. We have to look at the upcoming week—and really, the upcoming month—and plan around the disruptions.

(I didn't put the all-day event on my calendar. My fault. I was depending on someone else to put it on the group calendar. That didn't happen. Still hasn't happened. But I should have whipped out my phone and sent myself a note. Life lesson here! Don't depend on other people to record the upcoming schedule. Head-slapping moment!)

Lesson 43: When we know writing is impossible on a planned day, we can flip that day out with a creativity / planning day or a rest day.

Today, I flipped my project writing and this section of *Write a Book in a Month*. If you're following above, you'll see that it says 0,000 for the words today, and the total words hasn't been updated from yesterday. I can snatch increments of project writing later today, but I need my laptop and access to the internet for this section. I won't have that for today's ending hours. So, writing the current project comes last today. I may not achieve my 1,000 words today, but I have Friday and Sunday that may be possible to get the weekly word count. You will know tomorrow what I managed to do.

So, flipping inside a day is also a possibility. Just as I can have additional writing time, squeezed from somewhere else.

Flipping the writing is simple. It just takes awareness.

Much of writing is about awareness: of our personal writing time, of our story world, and of the needs of those around us. We need to be aware of our commitments and obligations. When we are with those we love and when we are performing the tasks that keep us engaged with community and the jobs that pay the bills, we should be totally present rather than distracted.

Awareness helps us be totally present.

Writing is frustrating on its own. Characters won't let us push them around. The exciting action scene falls flat. The drama building in a relationship turns melodramatic. The words are stuck. Our minds won't settle. We run down alleys only to be faced with high brick walls.

Those commitments and obligations have their own frustrations. Sometimes, they create the interferences with our writing time—and perhaps even our writing mood. We have seasons when our writing time has to move to the backseat. You pick that length of time for the writing to be off-schedule.

Long blocks of time for writing are desirable but not necessary. We can crowd in a half-hour here and there or even several fifteen-minute increments. We can map out a scene while we drive. Or dictate—then plug in the headphones and transcribe it, building and adding and fixing.

The greatest problem with our writing time, the greatest problem with flipping is when we're dealing with toxic relationships.

Toxic relationships affect our ability to generate words and achieve our goals. Being mad when trying to write a joyful reunion, feeling worthless because some sociopath delights in tearing down the people around him: those situations aren't conducive to writing.

I have no solution for people who are involved in a toxic relationship. They have to decide. I do have questions for them, the chief of which is *how long*? Because toxic relationships don't improve.

Even in the worst seasons of our life, we should look ahead and see the coming of spring. I know. My horrible season lasted for years. In the worst of that horrible season, smothered with cold and dreary day after dreary day before me, those 15-minute increments were not even possible. That season did reach its end, however. I'm happier now than I've ever been. I'm achieving my long-term writing goals, delayed but now possible.

Lesson 44! Our chief concern should be our long-term writing goals. Yes, I know we want to write every day, all day long, but—there's life, you know. Whenever we have to flip around our schedules and flipping around our commitments and responsibilities, we do so with awareness of our long-term goals.

Have you considered what you will do when you finish this book you are writing? Do you only have one book in you? Or are you in it for the long haul?

Awareness of what you want and how you want it, those are the key. Flipping your devotion to what's important for your writing goals, that's the lock.

Insert key, open lock—walk into your dream.

April 19 ~ Input / Output

Current Project :: *To Wield the Wind*
Project Stage :: Sketching Ideas / Rough Shape
Yesterday's Word Count: 1,575
Today's Word Count: 1,100
Total Word Count: 21,798 / 33,000
Goal: 5,000 words per week
Weekly Words Achieved 5,670
Project Dates: March 25 to May 5 Publication

As promised, I have the totals from yesterday noted along with today's word count.

Yesterday, I managed an entire section of the novel, very late. Today, while in the back seat heading for errands, I had some great ideas and loosely sketched them. When I had a few spare minutes this afternoon, I got the sketch into a legible form before I forgot what I had written (because my handwriting and a moving vehicle don't mix).

I achieved my goal for yesterday and today, which means I have the goal for the week. This is great! I can focus on some proofreading tomorrow, heading to that all-day commitment that I mentioned earlier. Anything that I manage on Sunday will be bonus words.

Today, while riding back, after chattering for a while, another idea popped into my head: Input / Output, the title of this section.

Do you know what put that idea in my head? Our usual complaints about people trying to text while driving. That started a thinking chain. Do people think anymore? Do people spend any time with just their minds? Or do they have a constant need to have static going on, whether that static is music or talk radio or game apps or texting or tweeting or whatever else they have to do—instead of being in the present?

When do we have time to think? Time to let our minds have a conversation with us? Time to let our minds think and give us ideas?

Many people don't seem to think at all. They just react. Even their supposed actions are reactions. Often, logic is not engaged, and everything is just emotion.

A writer can't be only emotion. Logic is necessary to craft stories. Lesson 45.

Mulling over the drivers who are texting and the people who gripe at store clerks and the parents who are busy on their phones rather than with their children—all of these brought me to another aspect of the writer's life: the whole of the writer's life ~ body and heart, soul and mind. Here comes the multi-part Lesson 46.

Our input for our body affects our writing. Nutrition and exercise help our writing thrive in unbelievable ways. A sugar-filled, highly processed diet dulls down our entire physical system while a balanced diet with proper protein, complex carbs, and the good fats bolsters every part of our body. Exercise gets our blood and oxygen pumping, equally necessary for our brains, where the creative muse and the critical editor live.

Our heart can thrive when relationships bring the input of love and belonging and support. Music should lift our emotions rather than grind us down with raging sound. Entertainment should give us joy and feed our curiosity and soothe the disturbances of the everyday world. Our conscious output should be a re-connection with the natural rather than a separation through the mechanical and electrical.

When we commune with others, when we meditate on the universal good, when we acknowledge our wrongs and strive to improve ourselves and others, the synergies of the input/output sequence enrich our souls. Whether faith or philosophy or a religious connection, we recognize our smallness in the great tome of time. Our syllable-sized[2] lives might appear to have little impact in the grand story of eternity, yet tiny ripples affect others far beyond what we can imagine.

In looking at the dynamic of input/output, we know that our minds need this synergy just as much as the other parts of our selves do. For artists (and writers are artists with words), the synergistic flow has greater needs. We crave input just as much as output. The wrong input, however, interferes with the output. Offer the mind a mental diet of junk, and the mind will output junk.

"We are what we eat," someone coined a long time ago, about the same time that someone else coined, "No pain, no gain."

We can just as easily say, "We are what we think. We are what we do." If you want to improve, no gain is possible without a painful cutting away of the bad.

It's a simple formula. Cut the bad, live the good. Whether it's processed food or couch-laziness, whether it's toxic relationships or dulling binge-tv, whether it's arrogance or lust, or whether it's sensation rather than sense, bad input brings only bad output.

Be in the present—even when driving the car.

Be in the present—cook the food you eat rather than zapping it. Enjoy the world you're walking through.

Be in the present—bolster your loved ones. Connect with your colleagues. Spread peace into the stressed world around you.

Be in the present—know who you are *and* who you aren't. Have realistic expectations even as you

---

[2] William Shakespeare was the first writer I know of who talked about syllable-sized lives, in the famous speech from *Macbeth*: "Tomorrow and tomorrow and tomorrow . . . to the last **syllable** of recorded time." He has various metaphors for our individual lives in this speech, one of which eternity is a book and our lives are a single syllable in that book. Some syllables make sense on their own; some need other syllables to make sense. Have your syllable make sense on its own.

work to improve the spheres you enter daily.

Be in the present—rather than trying to live distracted.

I sound a little like a 60's hippie who believes in flower power. Or a guru preaching the twelve-fold way to serenity.

It's Good Friday. The greatest redemptive act occurred today. What small redemptive act can you do to improve your writing?

Be in the present.

April 20 ~ Looking Ahead

Current Project :: *To Wield the Wind*
Project Stage :: Planning
Today's Word Count: 0,000
Total Word Count: 21,798 / 33,000
Goal: 5,000 words per week
Weekly Words Achieved 5,670
Project Dates: March 25 to May 5 Publication

I didn't plan for any creative writing today. I couldn't have even if I wanted to do so. On the long drive down and back for the family gathering, I worked on manuscript corrections while in the back seat. (*Not* the current project.)

And I am *tired*. I'm an introvert; people exhaust me.

So, after reaching home, cleaning up, getting irritated at my baseball team, and finally heading off to post tonight's blog, I decided to look at the sketch that I worked out on Friday and see how many days I would need to write those scenes for the last third of *To Wield the Wind*.

All I can say is this: Yikes!

According to my projected sketch, I have 12 scenes remaining. It takes a day per scene, sometimes two. I don't have 12 days—not if I want to achieve the deadline of May 5 Publication.

I have fifteen days, but I'll need a couple of days for final revisions and corrections. Definitely Yikes time.

So, I must buckle down for double-duty days. The *rough shape* has to move into the *draft*.

The *rough shape* takes sketched ideas and turns them into scenes and sequels. I form up sections or chapters. With the sketch as a guide, I develop dialogue and events with a rapid-flow write than cycle back to fill in and fix up. Plot holes and character discrepancies are fixed. While the sketch is white-hot creativity uncontrolled, the rough shape is creativity controlled.

In the *draft*, I fix any problems that I might have skipped while I ensure the manuscript elements are correct (format, spelling, etc.). The draft is a mix of creative muse and critical editor—and the muse usually loses to the editor. It's the third look at the story—although really, the sketch is only a glimpse.

After the draft, I head into corrections, usually reading the manuscript backwards.

To meet my goal it will be double-duty from here on: rough shape *and* draft on the same day.

I might have over-estimated the word count for some scenes; that would help. However, I must devote just as much writing focus to these ending chapters as I devoted to the beginning ones.

While this book is not a cliff-hanger—I will resolve issues for this story—it is the first of a trilogy. The primary antagonist will not be defeated until the final book. These final 12 scenes are chockful of intriguing and angsty problems to attract readers to the second and third books.

So, here's the schedule I need to follow. Every day after drafting, I will need to proofread and make corrections.

FINISHING THIS WEEK

Sunday 4/21 ~ Rough: 1,000 > 22,800 / Draft: 2,000 > 2,000

NEXT WEEK

Monday 4/22 ~ Biz required / Take Note required / Draft: 3,000 > 5,000

Tuesday 4/23 ~ Errands / Rough: 1,000 > 23,800 / Draft: 2,000 > 7,000

Wednesday 4/24 ~ Commitment in the evening / Rough: 1,000 > 24,800 / Draft: 2,000 > 9,000

Thursday 4/25 ~ Rough: 1,000 > 25,800 / Draft: 2,000 > 11,000

Friday 4/26 ~ Commitment required / Rough: 500 > 26,300 / Draft: 3,000 > 14,000

Saturday 4/27 ~ Rough: 1,000 > 27,300 / Draft: 2,000 > 16,000

Sunday 4/28 ~ Commitment required / Rough: 500 > 27,800 / Draft: 2,000 > 18,000

FINAL WEEK

Monday 4/29 ~ Rough: 1,000 > 28,800 / Draft: 2,000 > 20,000

Tuesday 4/30 ~ Errands / Rough: 1,000 > 29,800 / Draft: 2,000 > 22,000

Wednesday 5/1 ~ Commitment in the evening / Rough: 1,000 > 30,800 / Draft: 2,000 > 24,000

Thursday 5/2 ~ Rough: 1,000 > 31,800 / Draft: 2,000 > 26,000

Friday 5/3 ~ Commitment required / Rough finished > 33,000 / Draft: 3,000 > 29,000

Saturday 5/4 ~ Draft: 4,000 > 33,000 / Complete Read-through, frontwards

Sunday 5/5 ~ One last read-through, backwards then Publish.

Oops, I see a problem already. I need to write the back-copy blurb. I might squeeze that in on a Friday.

Oh, shoot. I see another problem. We've got a trip planned for May 3rd through 5th. I have to finish WAY BEFORE May 3. I need to shift the target to May 1st.

It's possible. On several days I've written more than the required 1,000. Finishing the *rough* shape needs to be the focus. Finishing that means that I can possibly do 5,000 drafted words in a day. That would greatly help!

Let's see how tomorrow goes. I'll refocus the schedule every Monday and Thursday. But I might not make a 33,000-word novel in 35 days. Remember, I just lost 5 days.

Victoria Holt, I have to emulate you!

And no real lesson for today.

April 21 ~ Short Post

Current Project :: *To Wield the Wind*
Project Stage :: Rough Shape
Today's Word Count: 1,912
Total Word Count: 23,710 / 33,000
Goal: 5,000 words per week
Weekly Words Achieved 7,582
Project Dates: March 25 to May 5 Publication

A short post tonight, just an update. As noted yesterday, I realized that I had 12 scenes still to write. I accomplished one of those tonight—along with a tricky little twist that was totally unexpected for me.

11 scenes to go.

Less than 10,000 words remain—the scenes will now determine the word count. I will continue to keep up with the tally. Keeping my fingers crossed!

April 22~ Biz Monday

Current Project :: *To Wield the Wind*
Project Stage :: Draft
Today's Word Count: 5,250
Draft Word Count: 5,250 / 33,000
Goal: 15,000 words per week

Current Project :: *To Wield the Wind*
Project Stage :: Rough Shape
Today's Word Count: 0,000
Total Word Count: 24,810 / 33,000
Goal: 5,000 words per week
Weekly Words Achieved 0,000
Percent of Project Completed :: 75%
Project Dates: March 25 to May 5 Publication

Update

When I *Looked Ahead* on Saturday, I realized that 12 sections remained. I wrote one of the 12 on Sunday, leaving 11 to go.

Those 12 sections will turn into about six chapters ~ one written Sunday, leaving 5 to go. These sections are very important. They will wrap up this book as well as set up the entangled conflict for the next book and the disentangling conflict for the third book.

That's approximately 10,800 words, with 1,912 on Sunday, leaving 8,888 to go.

If I don't make publication by May 2—I have a trip, remember—then I'll finish and publish on May 8.

That will put me three days behind for the next book. Deadline missed. After last year's blown deadlines for two books, I don't like being behind. Sigh.

Today's Focus

I had three things on my To-Do List: 1] Take Note, 2] Biz Monday, and 3] reaching the 5,000-word mark on the *WieldWind* draft. I didn't get to the draft yesterday, so I had to push today.

I achieved my goals for today—but I had to cry off on a couple of fun activities.

Today is Biz Monday.

I've had Bills Monday and Promo Monday already this month. Biz Monday focuses on the business of writing. Schedule days for personal bills and promos and writing biz each month—and don't neglect them.

When I started publishing in 2016, I neglected two very important aspects of the writing business: ISBNs that I control and copyright registration.

The law says that a written work of any sort is copyrighted as soon as it is complete. "Poor Man's Copyright" is mailing the manuscript to yourself to get the postmarked date and not opening that package. However, a recent Supreme Court ruling says that writers who want to prosecute people who steal copyrighted work must have that work officially copyrighted.

I considered working on copyright last year, but it was too easy to put it off. The world had a couple of events as proof that it was *Time to get copyrighted officially*. But I shifted the whole process to the back burner.

I procrastinated because of the cost. If I hadn't procrastinated, I would likely have saved money. That's the way with life—put things off and pay later.

This year I probably would have continued to procrastinate, but a couple of things drove me to move ahead: the #copypastecris scandal and the Supreme Court ruling lit a fire in me. I learned, a long time ago, that I get two warning events before a third cascades trouble over me.

So, completing copyright registration moved to the front burner—as soon as I had spare cash.

The spare cash came when I completed my taxes. My refund—which usually goes for fun things (refund fun, you know)—would pay for the ISBNs and copyright registrations for most of my published books—which isn't very many for Remi Black, but I also have two other pseudonyms.

Starting through the process of copyright registration, I hoped to wait on the ISBNs, only to encounter a portion of the form that asked for the ISBN associated with the book. Off I go to Bowker and purchase my first ISBNs, 10 at a time. I filled out those forms then moved to the copyright registration.

I will say that Bowker and the Library of Congress (in charge of US copyright) have made the task easy—unless you have lots of forms to fill out. Sigh.

Getting every published book through the process will take more than my refund, but I've started now and will finish. As of this publication, every title is current on ISBNs and copyright.

The process is not fun. It's tedious. It entailed re-writing several blurbs to get them to the required 350-word length on Bowker—which meant that I also took care of another procrastinated job. Some of those early blurbs were not well written. I've learned a lot about marketing since 2015 and 2016 and those first 10 books.

Now that everything is basically current, I'll keep ISBNs "banked" and apply for copyright registration whenever I finish a new manuscript.

The publish part of the writing business will be Finish MS > Write Blurb > Have ISBN Ready > Publish > Connect to Author Page > Announce with Promos > Apply for copyright. Then it's off for the next book adventure.

So, Lesson 47 ~ Don't procrastinate on the protections of your intellectual property.

Copyright is a necessity. ISBNs are necessary for copyright--people may argue with this one, but I'm not certain they've actually read the forms. Don't procrastinate too long. A cascade of troubles could crash over you. Tedious is not fun but necessary. Be careful as you file.

April 23 ~ Master Book

Current Project :: *To Wield the Wind*
Project Stage :: Draft
Today's Word Count: 2,208
Draft Word Count: 7,458 / 33,000
Goal: 15,000 words per week

Current Project :: *To Wield the Wind*
Project Stage :: Rough Shape
Today's Word Count: 2,145
Total Word Count: 26,955 / 33,000
Goal: 5,000 words per week
Weekly Words Achieved 2,145
Project Dates: March 25 to May 5 Publication

Ever read a book where the character's name changed halfway through? Or the eye color changed? Or a past event gets reported wrongly later in the book?

These discrepancies can be usually be avoided with a Master Book ~ Lesson 48.

For *To Wield the Wind*, I started the Master Book today. I'm over 75% through the roughly shaped manuscript, and I'm only now starting the Master Book.

I've been a naughty writer. 😉

A Master Book, sometimes called a Bible, is the collection of basic facts about characters and setting and plot. Here's the place that you record specifics of character appearance, the details of important locations, and the events of each chapter.

Most people fill their Master Book with researched information.

For the book that gave me fits last year, *The Key for Spies* under my pseudonym M.A. Lee, I had notes about the Spanish and Basque language, copies of information about Wellington's Peninsular Campaign in Spain during 1813, information about musketry and soldiers' uniforms in the British and French armies, recipes for typical Spanish dishes, and much, much more. Some of the information was research prior to starting the book; most of it came about as I wrote it. Research for a few things happened only as they spilled into the manuscript.

Smart writers keep the Master Book as a ready reference even after they finish the manuscript. They know that they might return to the characters and the world already built. They might have no immediate plans for return, but the Master Book waits, ready for use.

I didn't start the Master Book for *Wield Wind* when I would normally have done so, from the first moment of conceiving the story.

One primary reason for the delay is that I was busily working on other books.

Since I was working with a fantasy world that I am greatly familiar with, I knew that research wouldn't be necessary.

To Wield the Wind is much more fantastical than the other books set in the Enclave World. I would be adding elements totally new to the series. I had a general idea of the new creatures and powers that would be needed. I figured I could keep those in my head.

I've had to do a lot of flipping back and forth, however, checking details, that a Master Book would have prevented.

The second primary reason for not creating the Master Book is that I just wanted to see what would spring upon the stage, gifts from the creative muse. To create the Master Book prior to the rough shaping process might "set in stone" certain details that the muse, in all her impishness, might change.

And the muse *did* change things. She deepened others. Basic facts haven't changed, but the whys and wherefores of those facts have. If I had set the elements in place, the muse wouldn't have played around in my head.

So I'm grateful to the muse, but as I approach the end of the roughly shaped manuscript, it's time to write information down.

As I revise following a day's drafting, I record what I come across. Today, I recorded yesterday's work.

Today started with shoveling a little dirt for a vegetable garden. Then I came in for the rough shape. By mid-afternoon, my work transitioned to the draft. Early supper had to be cooked, a softball game had to be rooted for, and this blog had to be written.

But it's been a great day for writing. Let's see how tomorrow will go.

April 24 ~ Expect the Unexpected

Current Project :: *To Wield the Wind*
Project Stage :: Rough Shape
Today's Word Count: 0,050
Total Word Count: 27,005 / 33,000
Goal: 5,000 words per week
Weekly Words Achieved 2,195
Project Dates: March 25 to May 5 Publication

After gleefully anticipating three blocks of writing time for Wednesday, I found my entire day disrupted, one event after another.

Morning / Afternoon / Evening ~ all lost.

These are not the distractions from the April 4th blog, "Nix Distractions." Distractions mean that you have writing time; you just don't write, for multiple reasons. Disruptions are completely different. Disruptions prevent the time for writing.

Various things cause disruptions. Necessary errands are part of the normal schedule. Unexpected accidents—car wrecks, dog lodging stick in throat, onset of flu—these make it nigh on impossible to get any words while you're dealing with them.

Many disruptions can be welcome. Friends drop in unexpectedly. Opportunities for fun show up.

Disruptions are the reason that writers can't stop as soon as they hit the goal mark: they have to continue until they finish the flow of the day.

I don't begrudge the disrupting events that happened today.

It's just—they kept occurring!

I accepted the morning loss and thought, "Okay, hit it this afternoon."

Only to lose the afternoon. I kept smiling even though the interruptions kept disrupting—can I count 50 words as progress? I'm going to. That's 50 more words than I had this morning.

And I did get a lot of thinking done.

Lesson 49 ~Disruptive days happen. 1] Count what you can. 2] Ponder problems whenever possible. 3] Keep smiling. 4] Hit it fresh tomorrow. 5] Don't stop writing just because you hit the goal mark.

April 25 ~ *Carpe Diem* for Writers

Current Project: *To Wield the Wind*

Writing Stage: Rough Shape

Today's Word Count: ~~ Total Word Count: / 33,000

Goal: 5,000 words per week > Weekly Words Achieved

Project Start Date: March 25

Projected End Date: May 5 Publication

Current Project :: *To Wield the Wind*
Project Stage :: Draft
Today's Word Count: 3,330
Draft Word Count: 10,788 / 33,000
Goal: 15,000 words per week

Current Project :: *To Wield the Wind*
Project Stage :: Rough Shape
Today's Word Count: 2,925
Total Word Count: 29,880 / 33,000
Goal: 5,000 words per week
Weekly Words Achieved 5,120
Project Dates: March 25 to May 5 Publication

Just as we writers have unexpected disruptions (yesterday for me), we also have unanticipated bonuses (today!).

We need to use these times wisely (Lesson 50) to recover whatever time we have lost and may and will lose ahead.

Writers cannot drift. We have to seize these offered days.

ROUGH SHAPE: Yesterday I needed 1,000 words and only achieved 50 = 950 lost. Today I needed 1,000 and achieved 2,925 = Gain!

DRAFT: Yesterday I lost the whole 2,000 needed. Today I needed 2,000 more = 3,330 (700 lost in the two-day span).

I will look for upcoming opportunities to retrieve those 700 words.

UPDATE

Monday 4/22 ~ Biz required / Take Note required / Draft: 5,250 > 5,000 = Success

Tuesday 4/23 ~ Errands / Rough: 1,000 > 23,800 = 2,145 Success
  Draft: 2,000 = 2,208 Success > 7,000 = 7,458 Success

Wednesday 4/24 ~ Commitment in the evening / Rough: 1,000 > 24,800 = 50 Failure
  Draft: 2,000 = 0,000 Failure > 9,000

Thursday 4/25 ~ Rough: 1,000 = 2,925 Success > 25,800 = 29,880 Success
  Draft: 2,000 = 3,330 Success > 11,000 = 10,788 less than 200 words Off Track

Friday 4/26 ~ Commitment required / Rough: 500 > 30,300 / Draft: 3,000 > 14,000

Saturday 4/27 ~ Rough: 1,000 > 31,300 / Draft: 2,000 > 16,000

Sunday 4/28 ~ Commitment required / Rough: 500 > 31,800 / Draft: 2,000 > 18,000

Final Week

Monday 4/29 ~ Rough: 1,000 > 32,800 / Draft: 2,000 > 20,000

Tuesday 4/30 ~ Errands / Rough: 1,000 > 33,800 Finished?
  Draft: 2,000 > 22,000

Wednesday 5/1 ~ Commitment in the evening / Rough: ??? / Draft: 3,000 > 25,000

Thursday 5/2 ~ Draft: 4,000 > 29,000

Trip > May 3 to 5

Monday 5/6 ~ Draft: 3,000 > 32,000

Tuesday 5/7 ~ Errands / Draft: 1,000 > 33,000 / Complete Read-through, frontwards

Wednesday 5/8 ~ One last read-through, backwards then Publish.

Deadline missed by three days.

I'm still planning to push!

April 26 ~ Nose to the Grindstone

Current Project :: *To Wield the Wind*
Project Stage :: Draft
Today's Word Count: 3,487
Total Word Count: 14,275 / 33,000
Goal: 15,000 words per week

Current Project :: *To Wield the Wind*
Project Stage :: Rough Shape
Today's Word Count: 0,000
Total Word Count: 29,880 / 33,000
Goal: 5,000 words per week
Weekly Words Achieved 5,120
Project Dates: March 25 to May 5 Publication

Today's goal was 500 words on the Rough Shape, but my commitment took longer than expected—more unexpectedness (see the April 24 blog).

Today's goal on the Draft was 3,000 words. I managed 487 more than that, nearly half what I lacked yesterday.

Like an inchworm, I'm achieving the goal. However, the end date is rapidly approaching. The upcoming trip will interfere. The forgotten and now reminded commitment for Saturday will also interfere. But I'll reach my goal of publication in May, whether that's before the 5th, on the 5th or the 8th or the 10th.

Then what?

Well, I've started mining ideas for the next book. I had a Sunday a couple of weeks back when I needed a thinking break for the creative muse. I set aside this project and let myself consider the next project. 1,300 words later, I have the strong seeds for a great story. I've already contacted my cover designer. The cover will be available around the time that I start writing the story—which should be a wonderful incentive to keep writing.

After publishing three books in three months, I thought that this project would be a chance to rest back a little and not push so much. Instead, a lot of unexpected disruptions have occurred. Spring is always a distraction. Summer, coming rapidly, is a ginormous distraction.

I should finish the next project in June followed by another project in August. I hope to use a nonfiction book as the break-away time for these two projects—rather than these nightly blogs that I've been writing.

The *following* project will be the farewell to a 12-book series of loosely connected stories set in the Regency period of England. *Mysteries and suspense with a dash of romance*, that's the tagline for the series. I've enjoyed this series.

Yet fantasy is my first love, and I hope to conclude the year with the two novellas that follow this project of *To Wield the Wind*.

I look at all this, and excitement fills me.

Some people would look at this and be overwhelmed.

I can achieve all of this if I keep my nose to the grindstone. Eleanor Hibbert (Victoria Holt, remember!) didn't consider her five-hours of writing every morning a grindstone-like chore.

When things are going well, I don't consider writing a chore either. It's a definite love, and I look forward to it.

People who still love writing or who are finding their way back to their love of writing, they've learned what to hate—and it ain't writing, folks ~ Lesson 51.

The ones that hate it, maybe they shouldn't call themselves writers. The ones who feel ground down by the desperate need to catch the next trend, to hack out the next story, to grab money rather than ideas, those can't be writers, can they? The ones who write what they're ashamed to name in the hunt for filthy lucre, those can't be writers, can they?

What did the old pulp writers call themselves? Hacks? They were putting out story after story, making good money, flipping around ideas, and doing it all for years and years. They enjoyed what they did. They *weren't* hacks. They were writers. They were prolific because they treated writing like a job.

They kept their nose to the grindstone—and didn't grind it away because they were doing what they loved ~ Lesson 52.

That's the goal. Grind to a fine silky flour that makes excellent cakes, pastry, yeast rolls, and biscuits. And stories.

April 27 ~ Writers' Groups

Current Project :: *To Wield the Wind*
Project Stage :: Musing
Today's Word Count: NADA
Total Word Count: 29,880 / 33,000
Goal: 5,000 words per week
Weekly Words Achieved 5,120
Project Dates: March 25 to May 5 Publication or May 8 or May 10

I'm not much for Writers' Groups.

There. I've said it. My prejudice is solidly up front. If you love your Writers' Group, don't continue.

If you have a love-hate relationship, read on.

Writers' Groups can be extremely helpful to newbies and gonnabees coming back into the dream after giving up for years.

The best ones give lots of practicable information and support for those who need the extra push to improve skills.

The worst ones devolve into social clubs and vain chest-pounding. Yes, you've been there, haven't you? We cringed together.

The larger gatherings, like conferences and long-weekend seminars, smash together quality and narcissism. Cost of the conference, the room, and travel can be prohibitive, so we have to weigh the outlay of funds with the perceived abundance of information. Sometimes the balance weighs in our favor; often, it doesn't. See, I'm being honest.

The local meetings trend to aspirations unfulfilled. Most locals don't have enough membership to weight the balance toward professionals. The local promotes critique groups as the primary method for skill improvement.

- Critique groups are hit-or-miss.
    - The successful ones start at the same level. Members all work hard for the goal of publication, and while they achieve it at staggered rates, they are achieving it.

- The unsuccessful ones start at varied levels with not one member published. Members bring in a chapter each month—and most members come erratically which means that few hear a longer story in its entirety. The critique, therefore, focuses on ticky details and misses the overall story arc.
- Collapsing critique groups give vicious responses designed to pamper the critiquer's self-esteem rather than improve the submitter's text. None are professionals. Members focus on denigrating published writers. They pick apart supposedly flawed sentences rather than look at the scenes and sequels.

If you manage to join a Writers' Group or a critique group with helpful pro writers, the newbies desperate for the rarefied air around a "real published author" turn into groupies rather than protégés. And the helpful pro writers, they usually only emerge for special occasions—because they're busy writing to meet a deadline.

Regional Writers' Groups—or those based in major metro areas—have the best chance of offering the information and support that writers need. These groups can draw a large enough membership to make the programs worthwhile. They generally are not specific to any genre—or the group is specific, but members fudge the meaning of genre just to have the sought-after interaction with other writers.

I once drove 2 ½ hours down and 2 ½ hours back to a monthly meeting in a metro area. The meetings leaned toward skill-building and network-creating information. I tried to get involved in a critique group, but no critique group within an hour of my residence was open to a newbie member. In the last months that I attended these monthly meetings—which were already becoming more and more difficult to manage—the meetings weren't very informative. One of the very last meetings that I attended had a supposedly high-brow Ivory Tower writer reading a story about pigs slavering for copulation with a boar. No, I'm not kidding. I'm not exaggerating. It was an unhappy half-hour.

I stopped going not long after that debacle.

Life took a bad turn, and I dropped out of the active writing scene for a decade. When I returned to writing, I tried to find a Writers' Group. I tried local. I tried a regional. I found better info online—and online help to seed the idea that I could participate in the ebook revolution and gave me professional writers to follow.

1] Floundering and flailing around, I stayed afloat. Personal networking does trump online interaction.

2] Venturing to the major writing group closest to my former home, I discovered Ivory Tower people. Acid-tongued critics. Bombastic wannabees. Nothing and no one on self-publishing.

3] I attended a couple of seminars but dropped out of the smaller groups, and the monthly meeting never fit with my work schedule. (Midweek and late, late, late—just like the critique groups.)

When I moved in 2017, I still tried to find a Writers' Group in my new area. I found the vanity people. I found the Ivory Tower worshippers. I found newbies trying to gain admittance to the Ivory Tower. I found wannabees rather than gonnabees.

A year and a half after my move, I may have finally found a group. I attended the three-hour initial meeting of a Sisters in Crime chapter. Primarily an informational meeting, the organizers left me with a great feeling that *this may be the one*.

We* shall see.

Keep writing goals in mind when seeking out a career-based group.

Don't go just to be going.

Listen only to the pros.

If you can't personally interact with pros, find the ones who give beneficial advice online.

Don't waste your money or your time. For writers, time is $$$ ~ Lesson 53.

*That's a Royal We.

April 28 ~ First Celebration

Current Project :: *To Wield the Wind*
Project Stage :: Rough Shape Finished!
Today's Word Count: 3,600
Total Word Count: 33,480 / 33,000
Goal: 5,000 words per week
Weekly Words Achieved 8,024

Current Project :: *To Wield the Wind*
Project Stage :: Draft
Today's Word Count: 542
Total Word Count: 14,817 / 33,000
Goal: 15,000 words per week

I'm celebrating.

After losing all of yesterday and knowing I was close, I focused on the rough shape today and finished it. Yes, finished! 3,600 words, which is what I should have written Friday, Saturday, and today. *Two days ahead of plan.*

The draft is nearly 1,000 words beyond where I expected it to be when I started looking ahead, one week ago. I'll be able to totally focus on the draft, revisions, and corrections for the next 3 days. I may make the original May 5 publication date, after all! That's most excellent!

That trip is still in the way. I still need to write the blurb. I have a couple of sentences, but I certainly need a bit more than that.

I'm in the final week that I originally projected. In looking at this week, I will have the usual errands and commitments along with an unexpected luncheon on Thursday with the trip still occurring on Friday.

I may hold the last of the revisions for the trip: I can revise in the car and 30 minutes here and there. Holding those, however, will mean a long correction session, so I *should try* to revise/correct as much as possible before packing and the luncheon on Thursday. Then I can let my creative muse and critical editor rest a bit before returning, finishing corrections, and publishing.

Publication may be on Monday, May 6. One day off-deadline is not as bad as three or five days off-deadline—and certainly not as bad as seven months off the deadline, which happened last year . . . and which also put another book off its deadline for five months and knocked two others completely out of the plan.

The end of April and the last day of this blog series is two days away. Check back for the celebratory publication blog.

Promo Plans for *To Wield the Wind*

I won't do any promotions for *To Wield the Wind* until all three novellas are published. Then I'll get ads for *Wield Wind* as well as do a special promotional trailer.

When all three books are out, I'll run 10 straight days of promos on Facebook and other social media sites.

I'll still haven't decided if I should do a bundle of the three books. I might wait on that until I have another trilogy gearing up for the Enclave World—I have ideas!

No lesson, but we don't need one, do we?

APRIL 29 ~ WRITERS CONFERENCES

Current Project :: *To Wield the Wind*
Project Stage :: Rough Shape FINISHED Draft at 65.9%
Today's Word Count: 7,250
Total Word Count: 22,067 / 33,000
Goal: 5,000 words per week
Project Dates: March 25 to May 5 Publication

Last August I attended a mystery writers conference. The specific one that I chose was Killer Nashville.

A couple of days back, I wrote about the benefits and detriments of monthly writers' groups. That blog reminded me that I haven't talked about the yearly conferences.

Writers Conferences are different from local writing groups. For one, you're surrounded by people who are intent on writing—or at least have enough money to pretend to be intent on writing. (You will occasionally run into the Ivory Tower literary writers [cue the upper-class posh accent] who are writing the next Great Novel but rarely accomplish more than 50 words in a year.) Information covers a wide variety of topics, all of which form the primary reasons to attend.

- character development and plot structure.
- genre tropes. For most mysteries, that means red herrings. Light comedy is needed for cozy mysteries.
- problems specific to genres (e.g., for fantasy: world building; for mystery: forensic evidence).
- marketing and promotions
- professional concerns like contracts
- the writer's life, such as avoiding burn-out
- pitch sessions with agents and editors.

If you've been intrigued about a conference, you should explore the conference information online before you decide to attend. Don't go based on someone's word.

For writers who have several books, and some of those are in print form, then go to the conferences designed for the fans, like Bouchercon in the mystery genre or the World Cons in the science fiction & fantasy genres. These are known as Readers Conferences or Fan-Based Conferences.

For writers of all sorts and in all genres, you need to attend a working conference. World Con is both fan and pro for SF/F. The Romance Writers of America have one of the best national conferences for any writer, pro and gonnabie pro. I've attended the famous Moonlight and Magnolias conference in Atlanta, hosted by the Georgia Romance Writers. My encounters with M&M have always been excellent.

Last year I was looking for a conference in the mystery genre. I had considered Malice Domestic, and while I was considering it, I stumbled across Killer Nashville, which I had never heard of

Killer Nashville! That's a great title, isn't it? I immediately investigated more.

This Nashville conference attracted me for several reasons:

1st, the conference has great reviews. In early 2019 it was named the Best Writers Conference by *The Writer* magazine.

2nd, the attendance at Killer Nashville is small enough not to be overwhelming but large enough to attract big-name authors who share their wisdom.

3rd, the panels hit a wide range of topics. Over six streams of panels often ran simultaneously, covering a range of topics for newbies, entry-level writers, mid-listers, and long-time pros smart enough to keep abreast of the field.

4th, the conference was in the mystery genre, which one of my pseudonyms focuses on. A couple of years back I realized that most books always have elements of mysteries (read: problems) to solve, especially fantasies.

5th, the conference is only about 2 1/2 hours away from my home. That's a drivable distance, which meant my only costs were the conference and the room. Plus food and gasoline.

2 ½ hours away, that's an afternoon's drive. However, I took the back roads getting there and turned that drive into 5 1/2 hours. That meandering drive wasn't an indication of the conference, however.

I scribbled down a lot of great pieces of advice which I've been putting into action. Here are only four, noted down during one panel discussion on Sunday morning.

- Eat the frog first thing in the morning.
- Record accomplishments as well as what you still need to work on.
- Do not write and revise at the same time. Creative flow is separate from critical flow.
- REV to recharge the creative spark: Read others / Exercise / Visit new people, places, things, and ideas.

I highly recommend going to a pro writers conference. This one started on Thursday noon and ended Sunday noon.

I've attended writers' meetings and seminars and a few other conferences. I find regional conferences work better for me. Local meetings are usually filled with newbies who give each other advice, with pro writers only occasionally appearing--unless they're desperate to toot their own horns. (Please read the April 27 post on Writers' Groups.) At conferences, the pros always appear.

Killer Nashville had a mix of writers of all experience levels as well as a mix of panels for those different levels. Great hotel, great people—although I spent all of my downtime writing. I considered the whole thing as a writing retreat, and that time away from my usual situation gave me the inspiration I needed to break through to several new ideas in the book that I was struggling with.

Writers Retreats are somewhat similar to conferences—without the multiple streams of panels, wide variety of people, and disparity of skill levels. Retreats focus discussions on skills and shared practices as well as appointed times for writing. Pros usually run the retreats and give the benefit of their experience. They conduct the retreat in settings conducive to creative energy—at beaches or in mountains or similar nature-based situations. A few retreats are held in high-energy locations, such as Vegas. The primary draw of a retreat is the pro's personal attention on each member of the cluster of writers.

Another type of Writers Retreat, the kind that attracts me, is a week away, totally focused on writing. Time for walks on the beach or trails, time for meals, time for musing on the deck or porch, and long blocks of time for writing. Having spent years craving those long blocks of time, I used to fantasize about a week at the beach or a week at a mountain cabin.

A] Investigate the conference. The $$ outlay can be significant. You need to factor reward against cost.

B] Find a conference that covers the topics that you need. Only attend the panels for those topics. Don't be swayed by other writers' needs.

C] Use your off-time wisely. Comments in panels will likely set your creative muse to jumping about. You can find quiet places to allow the muse to pour out those new ideas if you're prepared.

D] Know what you want from the conference. You might want a retreat instead.

E] Be open to new ideas and new ways of thinking about your writing. Pick a handful to put into practice upon your return home. Don't shove your notes over to one side and forget about them.

F] (which L5 hinted at) Be amiable. You don't have to be gregarious.

Lesson 54 ~ Try a Writers' Conference or Retreat to re-charge.

April 30 ~ An End that's not an End

Current Project :: *To Wield the Wind*
Project Stage :: Rough Shape FINISHED Draft at 84%
Today's Word Count: 6,137
Total Word Count: 28,204 / 33,000
Goal: 15,000 words per week
Weekly Words Achieved 13,387
Project Dates: March 25 to May 5 Publication

Today is the last official entry in this series.

We've covered a lot.

- Importance of Planning: 4/2, 4/3, 4/9, 4/14, 4/18, 4/20, 4/25
- Interferences and How to Overcome them: 4/4, 4/5, 4/6, 4/13, 4/21, 4/24, 4/26
- Tracking to Stay Successful: 4/7, 4/11, 4/12, 4/17, 4/19, 4/28, and today
- Knowing the Biz of Writing is more than Writing: 4/10, 4/15, 4/16, 4/22, 4/23, 4/27, 4/29

And that's certainly not everything. We've had all these lessons and more.

None of it, however, covers a writer's need for practical knowledge: story discovery, plot structure, character development, sentence craft, author branding.

This practical knowledge is highly essential, but it was never the focus of this series. The struggles and mindfulness necessary to overcome these struggles, that was our key focus.

Knowing what your dream is, pursuing it daily rather than going away from it: that's mindfulness.

An early mantra that helped me move from *wannabie* to *gonnabee* and now to *being*: Dream it. Believe it. Do it.

Dream it.

1] Deciding your dream

2] Envisioning your specific goals

3] Planning the reality of where you will be

BELIEVE IT.

1] Going after it actively rather than just thinking about it

2] Choosing to start, choosing the writing over mindless behaviors.

3] List quantifiable and achievable goals rather than nebulous ones.

DO IT.

1] Overcoming the goal-disrupting life rolls.

2] Staying devoted through stress and weariness and sickness and depression.

3] Researching whatever it takes to turn your writing to the end result: a book, in your hands, tangible and real.

When you hold that book, you realize the sacrifices are worth it.

And then you do it all over again ~ Lesson 55.

From the beginning of this Writer's Month, I knew I would not finish on this 30th day of the month. I was writing 40 days, not 30. I started five days early; I have five days to go—at minimum.

Check back on May 5th for an update on publishing then again on May 15th when I lay out the actions I take after clicking the e-book button that says "Publish".

May 5th ~ 1st Post-Draft Update

Current Project :: *To Wield the Wind*
Project Stage :: Rough Shape FINISHED Draft FINISHED on May 1st Current Stage :: Proof-Plus
Word Count on May 1st: 7,687
Total Word Count: 35,891 / 33,000
Goal: 5,000 words per week
Weekly Words Achieved 1,800
Project Dates: March 25 to May 5 Publication

Honesty First

My original projected end date was May 5, at which time I would upload the e-book to an online distributor.

On Sunday, April 28, I mentioned that plans for the week would interfere with the May 5 publication date, but I thought I would be able to publish on May 6.

May 6 is still my goal.

I finished the draft on Wednesday (see above!) with a massive focus day: 7,600-plus words in one day. That's a lot!

Thursday was cooking, luncheon, and packing. My mind kept swirling with my pleasure with the end of *To Wield the Wind*. The ending scenes were so strong, too strong, to start Proof-Plus immediately. So, I had a nonfiction manuscript that I needed to head through Proof-Plus—a procrastinated job because I was so eager to start writing *Wield Wind*. I completed about 1/3 of that on Thursday evening.

Friday was driving to the destination and being there! Our cabin was cute. Our conversation was great! Our meals were excellent! In downtime I completed the 2/3 of the NF MS.

Saturday remained cute / great / excellent. I also finished the 3/3 of the NF MS.

The day after my start on the WWind draft, I had started the Proof-Plus. Then I had to start pushing to finish the rough shape and the draft, which meant the Proof-Plus was delayed. The first revision session reached page 23.

In the little bit of extra time on Saturday, I took the Proof-Plus to page 64 of the 144-page MS. I stopped because I was yawning too much. Clear heads are needed all through this stage.

It's mid afternoon on Sunday, May 5. Proof Plus is barely started. If I push the rest of today and all through tomorrow, I might—might!—make a midnight publication. We'll see.

WHAT IS PROOF PLUS?

Proof Plus contains several steps. Finishing the manuscript does not mean that a writer's job is done. We have to *complete* the manuscript.

Prepping for publication includes revisions (rapid-read followed by fixing holes and discrepancies). Then comes line editing (reading the MS backwards for errors) with corrections.

Insertion of front matter (title page, copyright notice, acknowledgements) and back matter (author's note, promos for other books) comes next. These are usually previously saved documents that are updated whenever I have new material.

The blurb is an old publishing term for the text promo copy. It's what you read on the back of the book that gives just enough of the story to intrigue and convince you to purchase the book. For online distributors, this is the book information page.

Blurbs are not easy to write. Tight writing is necessary. Marketing copy is completely different from fiction and nonfiction writing.

STEPS AHEAD

Rapid-Read: currently at page 64 of 144 pages

Fix: currently at page 64 of 144 pages (I usually Rapid-Read and Fix concurrently.)

Edit and Correct

Front Matter is already in; Back Matter is needed

Blurb

Publish

POST-PUBLISHING

Author Page Link

Basic Promotions and Advertisements

Video Trailer

Until all three books are out, only the author page link and the basic promotions will occur. I will save my advertising dollars until then, with *To Wield the Wind* running as a loss leader.

.~.~.~.

I am thrilled with the finished novella! Ideas popped in that I wasn't expecting: the creative muse certainly did her job on this one. Critical Editor is currently out to play. While I want to jump immediately to writing #2 and #3, I have other commitments to write first. Once those are out of the way, I will finish this trilogy.

Do come back on May 15 to catch what's happening with *To Wield the Wind*. Will I make my May 6 publish date, or will I have to back up to May 8?

Once I have the book up, the online distributor will send a link. The link starts the basic promotions.

Then the question becomes ~What's next in the pipeline—for Remi Black and for my other pseudonyms?

On with the Rapid-Read and Fix!

May 15th ~ 2nd Post-Draft Update

Here's the promised second update since finishing the draft of *To Wield the Wind*.

I missed the May 5 projected deadline for publication. As expected, that three-day trip allowed no access to my laptop to work on Proof-Plus. While on the trip, I completed revisions and fixes, but corrections were delayed until Monday, May 6.

Also, while on the trip, I sketched the bare ideas for the blurb, which is the promo copy for the book.

Monday, May 6

I worked first on the blurb. Writing market copy is completely different from writing fiction.

- Start the blurb with the tagline. As it set the tone for the book, it will keep the focus narrowed for the promo copy.
- Stay in present tense. This creates immediacy for the reader.
- Use Tight Writing. Here are the 3 quickest rules to show you TW ~ A] Avoid passive voice with the "by ~" prepositional phrases. B] Avoid any -ing verb forms. C] Avoid *there* as a sentence starter.
    - Avoid Passive Voice example: Orielle is viewed as prey by the magical creatures of the forest > The forest's magical creatures view Orielle as prey.
    - Avoid -ing example: She will be traveling to Iscleft Haven in order to renew the alliance between the Wizard Enclave and the Rhoghieri. > She travels to Iscleft Haven to renew the alliance between the Wizard Enclave and the Rhoghieri.
    - Avoid *there* example: There is a Dark Fae called Lady Bone who leads the Wild Hunt. > The Dark Fae Lady Bone leads the Wild Hunt.

Stay under 350 words, even with the two to three sentences at the end which place the book within the series and directs interested readers to your website.

After finishing the blurb, it was noon. I broke for lunch, fully expecting that the corrections would take until midnight or longer. Yet I managed to upload the corrected MS before 8 p.m. EST (DST).

Only one day off my projected deadline!

What have I done since Monday?

Here's Tuesday.

I received a link for the uploaded book. I checked it online—and found a major blooper. Fixed that.

On the weekend trip, I had proofed another MS, so I finished those corrections.

We've had this lesson: Keep other things going in addition to your primary project.

I created a promotional post announcing *Wield Wind*'s publication, containing the purchase link.

Paid bills (delayed from Monday) and took care of the volunteer writing, which usually runs 500-750 words.

Wednesday

With another primary project on the horizon, I shifted Promo Monday to this day. In addition to the regular posts, I set up scattered promos for *Wield Wind*: another announcement with link, promo with blurb and link, promo with first chapter and link.

These are passive posts. Following my plan, I will not have active, paid ads until all three novellas are out. This first novella will serve as the Loss Leader, hopefully driving readers to the next two novellas as well as the three 100,000-plus novels that are the main series for this world.

I haven't decided if I will bundle the three novellas. Right now, the pros and cons are running equal.

Finally, I updated copy and links for my Remi Black and main Writers Ink websites, both landing pages and author pages, to reflect the new publication. Try to keep the public presence up-to-date.

That's a long day of work. Monday, Tuesday, and Wednesday, all three were long days.

Thursday

Started research and the master book for my next project.

Basically, all work for *Wield Wind* is completed—unless I spot a major problem and until I start work for the next in the series, *To Charm the Wind*. No tinkering. Move on.

Friday to Wednesday, May 10 to 15

Nothing on *Wield Wind*. Just my normal stuff, with the same unexpected disruptions and tempting distractions, writing to do, projects to consider, and more and more.

So, I've completed the *Write a Book in a Month* Challenge. I was one day beyond my goal. 30,000 words in one month on one project while a second project is also ongoing is totally possible. I get fudge now! And who can turn down a little fudge?

I hope you find the 55 lessons and my experiences helpful and practicable for your own writing.

Lessons List

1 to 4] 4 Bees of Writing: realistic / time-aware / devoted / specific.

5] Look long-term.

6] Let ideas swirl for a while before acting on them.

7] Keep slogging.

8] Get joy by exploring another project.

9] Focus intensely only on one creative project.

10] Keep meeting the realistic goal.

11] Use an off day to think about upcoming scenes.

12] Know what to write.

13] Never write until dry.

14] Distance helps firm up ideas.

15] Keep sketched ideas handy.

16] Keep writing.

17] Know the business of writing.

18] Remember the obstacles to avoid their re-occurrence.

19] Daily goals drive the monthly and yearly one.

20] Track failures and successes.

21] Disruptions occur.

22] Story talks. Writers need to listen.

23] Specific goals help.

24] Take out what won't fit the schedule.

25] Do the calculations to understand realistic goals.

26] Kin, kith, and business keep us engaged with the world.

27] We can write anywhere.

28] When one project doesn't work out, turn to the next.

29] Keep the creative separate from the critical.

30] Creativity gives permission to be messy.

31] Eat the Frog first.

32] Tax-planning is essential for writers.

33] Writers are writing even when they're not writing.

34] We never know exactly what's coming, but we should still be present.

35] Readiness and awareness allow writing when we least expect to write.

36] Ideas come out of blankness.

37] Waiting won't kill the story.

38] Promotional posts.

39] A professional cover design is worth the cost.

40] Be familiar with the development and content of your own story; don't trust someone else to do it.

41] ISBNs and copyright fees are necessary expenses.

42] Keep moving on, writing the hard scenes as you reach them.

43] Flip an obstructed writing day with a creativity / planning day or rest day.

44] Our chief concern is the long-term writing goals.

45] Logic and emotion are necessary to craft stories.

46] We need to be in the present as body, heart, mind and soul.

47] Don't procrastinate on the protections of your intellectual property.

48] Discrepancies in story can be avoided with a Master Book.

49] Disruptive days happen.

50] Use all our writing time wisely to recover from disruptive days.

51] Know what it is you hate—and it shouldn't be the writing.

52] Keep your nose to the grindstone. You won't grind it away if you're doing what you love.

53] For writers, time is money.

54] Try a writers' conference or retreat to re-charge.

55] And do it all over again.

Enter the Writing Business

by

Edie Roones

Introduction

How do I succeed at writing? Most answers to that question focus on creativity ~ story development, character explorations, poetic contemplations, blogging topics, and more.

Business needs to be added to that list.

Refine the question ~ *How do I succeed at the writing business?*

Even our refined question can be divided into several.

- What are the best systems for writers?
- What are the best daily procedures?
- The best ways to balance creativity and practicality?

These are the first decisions to build a writing business.

Think of writing as running a small business. Writers create content ~ stories, poems, blogs, any of our writing. That content is our product to sell.

As creators of quality products, we have a Writing Biz.

Imagine a writing career. What is the reality? No, not the fantasy. What will the actual day-to-day writing life be? Daily writing requires that we find ways to cope with the soul-suckers who interfere with your creative energies.

Enter the Writing Business offers the reality of the writing career. This guidebook is a series of posts on the daily creative process and the daily devotion to writing before it transitions to business decisions. We look at the necessary writing space then the essential hard and soft skills. To succeed, though, we need a business plan designed for writers. That biz plan will direct our daily actions, weekly plans, and monthly reviews and previews :: the Do's that few consider until swamped by the constant Do-ing of them.

This guidebook is more than a tossed life preserver. With the practicalities discussed here, you can avoid the swim across the channel and build a bridge to cross from newbie to pro writer.

As part of the five-year publication anniversary of my first book, I filled August 2019 with a blog series of thirty-plus basic decisions. The last two posts in the series chattered about the Hell and Heaven of Writing to answer every writer's constant unspoken question: *Is it worth it?*

Most new writers drop out before the five-year mark. I made many mistakes, but I have learned from them. Now I'm seeing better results every day, gradually building a list of books. I have creative plans and business plans. I'm no longer reacting; I'm taking well-considered actions.

Hopefully, by applying the lessons in *CA4W*, you can avoid those mistakes in reactions and expectations, and you will achieve success.

DREAM IT. BELIEVE IT. DO IT.

~ EDIE ROONES

1ST ~ WRITERS DREAM OF WRITING

August is anniversary month for Writers Ink, my writing business, gathering together all my writing under three pseudonyms.

- In August 2013, I decided to become *serious* about writing so I could make a living doing it.
- One solid year later, in 2014, I had finally changed a daily writing devotion guaranteed to achieve that decision. Self-discipline and devotion were difficult transitions.
- A year after, on August 30, 2015, I published my first book, on August 30, determined to get it out there before another Labor Day passed. October 2015 saw three more novels published under a different pseudonym.
- Another year later, also in 2016 August I wrote my first business plan—about 9 months after I encountered this analysis of a small business' direction. Writing as a business :: a radical idea. To reflect the previous year's publications, I backed up the five-year biz plan to 2015. Maybe I should have backed it up to 2013, the actual decision year (with a few months preceding in 2012).

The Kindle began revolutionizing publishing in 2010. It wasn't the first e-reader; digital books had floated in the internet for years. The Kindle, though, reached the masses.

My first Kindle was a gift to myself for Christmas in 2012. Only in the summer of 2013 did my eyes open to the new doors available for writers. Although self-publication sounded worrisome, it was extremely tempting.

SLOW TO TRANSITION

One excuse for my slow comprehension of the changes in the publishing world was my brain-sucking job. Another is that I silently consider changes long before I implement them. Third, well, from 2004 to 2010, my life had several drastic changes that twisted my thinking the way a tornado wrenches trees. Sleep deprivation, depression, grief, emergency surgery—I barely kept my head above water, not losing my stuffing. I held onto my job, the one that paid all the bills. Gradually, I figured out a new perspective on life after focusing for so very, very long on others.

Major life changes can be like tornadoes, demolishing one area and leaving others seemingly untouched. Only after the devastation is over and clean-up begins will we discover how all areas are tied into the devastated one. Brain-sucking jobs can be ravaging to people desperate for personal creative expression even as those jobs offer helpful hard skills and soft skills.

This post, though, is about that first bullet and our first lesson ~

LESSON 1] BECOMING SERIOUS ABOUT WRITING

How often does anyone have the chance to achieve a lifelong dream?

1A] Dreams are not fantasies.

We all have fantasies. Becoming a player on a major sports team. Winning the Grammy for Best

New Vocalist. Looking super-model perfect all of the time. Winning the Lottery. Becoming a best-selling and wealthy writer.

Duke Ellington said, "A dream is a goal with a finish line."

1B] When a dream is a goal, that goal is attainable after effort over a span of time.

That span of time may last a year, three years, five years (which is the reason most business plans are five-year plans). The goal will have mid-term benchmarks based on short-term strategies.

When a dream is a fantasy, it plays and tinkers and feeds the ego. The long-term goal may look attainable, but whole elements of it are dependent on outside forces. Luck is an outside force. The best young athletes may never have a scout consider their potential. Backing from a music publisher can be a roll of the dice. It's expensive to have an air-brush makeup artist trailing behind you 24/7.

People fantasize about ideal lives all the time. Ideal is not real. It's pretty to look at, especially when we're slogging through the muck of daily life.

Goals with their long-term projects and benchmarks and strategies, those sound boring. The dream sounds like a job.

Becoming a writer, though ~ That sounds like a dream.

1C] A dream is a goal with legs.

You want to enable that dream for walking? You need to train the proper brain synapses in order to create locomotion.

You want to walk that dream? You have to train the muscles.

How do you train writing muscles?

Write. A daily drill of writing. Just like an athlete has a daily physical training drill.

Study. After all, perfect practice leads to perfect performance (or as close as possible).

Practice for that performance. Over and over.

Stephen Covey says, "Begin with the end in mind." Know the ultimate goal of your writing. What are you going to do with it? Choose ::

A] Keep it to yourself. You're just playing with writing, aren't you?

B] Aim for publication. Now you're in the story-telling business.

Be a great writing athlete. Just do it.

2ND ~ KNOW YOUR LIFELONG DREAM

WHEN DID YOU DECIDE TO BE A WRITER AS YOUR LIFELONG DREAM? LESSON 2]

I can remember the moment that I first wanted to be a writer. I had just finished a Phyllis A. Whitney novel. She wrote more than 70 in her long career.

Today we call Whitney's books vintage gothics. Her fellow giants in the genre were Victoria Holt and Mary Stewart (my favorite) and Dorothy Eden. The books are also called romantic suspense or woman in jeopardy.

I love reading. Devour anything read-able. My sister taught me to read before I started first grade—which was a good thing, or my reading skills would be like my math skills. Daddy called me a wiggle-worm, and first grade was a hard transition for me. Thanks to Diane, reading was and is my great love.

2A] Can a professional writer not love reading?

All those years ago, when I finished my first vintage gothic, I turned the last page and encountered Whitney's short biography. I know that I must have previously read other author bios. Whitney's note, though, struck me hard. I don't remember my thought process, but it must have gone like this:

- People write books > People make a living writing books > People make a living writing *interesting* books > I want to do that!

The dream was born.

2B] Wrangling the Lifelong Dream

For the next few years I played with stories.

Play is necessary. Children play at adult work. We learn what we like and don't like. Playing at writing, we discover our likes and dislikes.

The summer after the summer that my family's house burned to the ground, I completed my first story. This pitiful manuscript is in storage somewhere, less than 100 words and more than 50. I had impressed myself. (Rolled eyes, please.)

By college my reading had expanded, and I found my reading love, fantasy. Writers often write what they love to read.

I played with my first fantasy novel. My sister Diane even typed it for me. She also commented that all the "thous" and "thees" and "thys" and "thines" along with unusual words like *ululation* and *susurration* and *coruscation* and *crepuscular* created a difficult read. I acknowledged her advice but basically ignored it. "It's *my* book," I thought. "*I'm* in charge of *my* book, dammit."

Do you know the mistakes I made? Try "show-off." "Ego-driven." "Fantasist." Do those sound correct?

Read on for Lesson 3.

3RD ~ PURSUIT OF THE DREAM

My second completed manuscript had a lot of mistakes. Not typographical errors. Not grammar / usage / mechanics errors. Mistakes in handling the words. (My first completed MS was definitely juvenile in mindset by a juvenile).

LESSON 3] "A DREAM IS A GOAL WITH A FINISH LINE." ~ DUKE ELLINGTON

The major problem with my second MS was that I confused the fantasy of being a writer with the dream of being a writer and definitely with the reality of being a writer.

One mistake was thinking that finishing a manuscript was the finish line. Nope. Another was a mistaken belief in that manuscript's ability to match the quality of the books that I was reading. Third, the flaws with words prevented a flowing story. Nope!

Here are three essential questions to ask yourself about every story you tell.

3A] Should the writing interfere with the story?

My fascination with archaic language (thee / thou / thy / thine) and archaic language forms (doth / hast) as well as a need to add in fancy words like *coruscation* and *susurration* doomed that iteration of the story.

Writers can have touches of beautiful and lyrical and fun on every page of a manuscript.

We can use touches of archaic language to distinguish a particular character through speech.

We can touch in a few $50.00 words to spark a little curiosity in the reader.

The key word is *touches*.

As soon as poetic or archaic language or vain vocabulary overwhelms the page, we overwhelm the story, obscuring it for the reader who merely wants entertainment.

We should invite readers into our stories, not drive them away.

3B] Whose story is it?

Remember, I considered that story—*The Tower of Lannoge*—to be mine! I crowded fancy words and language onto every MS page. I burdened the story with a title that really had very little to do with the book.

I did a great disservice to the story.

The story belongs to itself, not to an individual writer. We just craft our version of the story (for which we will acquire copyright and receive payment).

Deliberately crafting a difficult read pleased no one but myself. In the publishing world of the time, I could have paid a vanity publisher to send my book into the world. Fortunately, the money wasn't in my banking account for that frivolous emptiness.

However, I did and could scrape together the money for postage. I sent that pathetic MS to every appropriate publisher in the annual *Writers' Market*. One year, two years, and three before I admitted the story was flawed at the basic word level. Then I launched into the first major revision. (The "Revision Hell" blog will follow later in this month, along with another on how to know when to give up on a MS.)

3C] What are my intentions with this story?

Even after three years of rejections, my life-long dream remained "make a good living writing interesting books". Fiction writers are story-tellers, first and foremost.

All that archaic and fancy language destroyed any interest in that story, a key element of my dream. I over-crafted at the basic level of story. All to please myself.

My claim of "my book, dammit" is only accurate if I *never* wanted to send the book into the world. I certainly did—which meant the book was intended for everyone, not me.

I continued to have struggles with this lesson on intentions. I've learned, finally, that story should flow unhindered while revision to story should only enhance the story's flow. My ego has nothing to do with the words on the page. These are now two of my goals for every story I write: the third is to make it interesting.

These three mantras are the start for every writer.

- Serve the story, not your own ego.
- Write to communicate, not for vanity.
- Know the goal, not the fantasy.

4ᵀᴴ ~ Laser-Eyed Writing

Becoming serious about writing requires a laser-eyed focus. Lesson 4]

"Laser-eyed focus" is a phrase used by the financial guru Dave Ramsey of *Financial Peace* whose money-budgeting system is similar to the envelope system. Ramsey and the envelopes are successful because both systems *control* all money coming in.

For people who want to get out of debt and stay out of it, the system helps you determine the amount of InCome ($ coming in), the amount of OutGo ($ paying bills), and the amount of wiggle-room disposable. Using the disposable wisely means paying down the debt with the highest interest rate first. Once the first debt is paid off, the laser-eyed focus turns to the next then the next until all debts are paid.

Too many people fall into the debt trap by living above their means. They choose a lifestyle, not reality (another instance of fantasy creating problems in the real-world).

- Want to go on vacation? Decide how much money is necessary. Save it so you can pay cash.
- Seeing the physical dollars leave your hand encourages careful spending. With plastic, we never see the money leave. Some of us don't even look at the receipt.
- Some people take a side job and chunk all of that cash onto the debt, dropping it down faster. Or they use the side-job money to fund their frivolous expenses, like vacation.

Do you know what writers fantasize about? Quitting the day job and writing during all those hours previously devoted to the job. We think "Would I Be Better Off Writing?" The answer is "Yes." The wallet and our bills say "No!".

Money is a resource that demands careful expenditure. Writers need to monitor closely any spending of their earned income.

4A] Be Money-wise.

Some of the writers who profited in the early days of the Kindle Revolution did so because few books were available in the marketplace. Their books sold and sold and sold, making them a mint. They quit their jobs and spent and spent and spent rather than saving. More stories soon entered the marketplace. A greater supply created competition for story-buying dollars. These writers of the early Kindle days saw their incomes shrink drastically.

Apply reality to the fantasy. Yes, for your writing career, you would be better off writing rather than heading to the 9/5 office, especially if you have a boss who wants you on-call 24/7. However, you need money. You need your emotional support. WIBBOW[3] comes after these two. Don't quit the day job until a guaranteed $$$ supply is available, a supply not dependent on market forces (like over-supply).

---

[3] An acronym, coined by Scott William Carter, which means "Would I be better off writing?" For 99% percent of the questions, the answer is "yes!"

4B] Keep the Circle Strong

Family can turn into a brood of beloved vampires. Even as you love and enjoy them, children can drain all of your strength. They have boundless frenetic energy. They have constant demands, infant to college-enrolled young adult. When you most need patience, they can drain all reserves.

Children are rewarding, though. They give you ideas, hope, love. Writers can find themselves chained by words; your loved ones will free you from those chains. We then wear the remaining links a little looser. The Circle is the most important goal, not a nebulous dream of the future. Even when your writing dream becomes a fulfilled goal, that evening spent with loved ones while playing rummy is still more rewarding goal than tapping the keyboard.

Spouses can be helpful supporters or hope-drinking passive-aggressive monsters. Writers have to remove TOXIC substances from their nests and carefully manage their resources (money, energy, emotions, time) to avoid pervasive spends by family. Supportive spouses look for ways to help. That's a two-way street. You have to support your spouse just as much. They have dreams, too.

Relationships are an obligation that we should enjoy and not mutely curse. Any obligation, like jobs, like families, will consume time, but it should not consume *all* of your time.

Babies and *littles* and *family in crisis* are different. They come first, always.

The Circle shares energy. One person can affect the whole group. Be the person who brings sunshine. Even when you don't feel like smiling, do so. That will affect your emotions as well as those around you.

4C] Support You and Yours Before the Writing

Every writer fantasizes about an InCome which means no more worries about how to afford writing—and china & crystal or beach vacations all through the winter, season tickets for the favorite baseball team or Super Bowl tickets every year, the great Hawaii escape or the modern-style home overlooking the lake.

Jobs—those things we have with bosses and the public—do create a steady and stable InCome, often with perks like health insurance and pensions. Yet those jobs can be vampires, drinking all your creativity and energy and inspiration. We *let* them drink everything. We have to juggle what's important to us > stable income vs. immediate pursuit of the dream.

Writers following the traditional publishing route have no guarantees. A contract doesn't guarantee the book will sell.

1. No guarantees that the writing will be accepted by a publisher.
2. No guarantees that the contracts will keep coming.
3. None that the advance will be sufficient.
4. Marketing and online presence still have to be funded.
5. Networking with readers and other writers still has to occur. Meetings, seminars, conferences, conventions, and more need funds.

Self-publishing can only guarantee that the book will enter the marketplace but no guarantees that it will sell. The costs can be budgeted::

1. Covers
2. Editing

3. Marketing
4. Online presence and networking

Even writers who have made a mint with their stories through film and licensing opportunities have no guarantee that the next book will retain their audience. If they do something totally stupid like p**s off a goodly portion of the population with an off-the-cuff comment, then they could lose any extra $$$ opportunities as well as their book audience.

4D] Time is Free

Time is the only free resource that writers can control.

The habit of the laser-eyed focus on writing can be difficult to build. It takes only 21 days to break a habit. It takes 66 days to build a habit. That's twice as long. The truth is that constructing something is infinitely more difficult than destroying it, as Bordon Deal shared in his story "Antaeus".

Awareness helps focus your laser eyes on your Writing Goal.

You can set up reminders to help you remember writing. You can convince family that a specific daily hour or two is devoted to writing, and then you'll come out and totally be with them. You can sneak an extra hour in the morning or the evening. You can use snippets of time for snippets of writing.

When you wisely use your spare time for writing, you don't begrudge your other obligations. The job becomes the means by which you pay for the opportunity to write, including taking a writing retreat to get over a difficult bridge in your story or online classes to improve your skills or to pay for better covers for your books. Family becomes a daily joy that pulls you out of your head. That interaction will improve the flow of ideas.

The habit of a regular writing time in a regular writing space has a greater benefit. Words come more rapidly. You find yourself musing over the story while you are away from your writing space, so that when you reach it, the words come pouring out. No more dread of the blank page.

That's right: writer's block becomes the nothing that it actually is.

5ᵀᴴ ~ Thunder! Lightning! Changes! Oh my!

During the interminable years of my intensive job, I often arrived home brain-weary, energy-zapped, and inspiration-less.

By the time I walked for exercise (which didn't happen as often as it should have) then fixed dinner and completed the essential chores, I didn't want to do anything but veg-out.

It took disgust and a time-based goal to remove the idea that I *deserved* to veg out. That disgust with doing nothing and hating the doing nothing while nothing still got done was key to developing my devotion to writing.

The disgust came one night in the late summer.

I was crocheting, working on a prayer shawl per month to donate to shut-ins. Crocheting is a soothing activity for me, mostly automatic except when I have to count for patterns. The shawls or lap throws all followed the same pattern; I didn't have to count, just hook the new stitch into the previous stitch and keep going.

If I wasn't crocheting of an evening, I was messing around on my new Kindle, purchased for my birthday in May. I had discovered the free classics and downloaded several. I found new writers. The Kindle was book browsing heaven, especially since my town had lost its local bookstore a decade earlier.

Usually, the Kindle was for weekend reading. On weekday evenings I would crochet while I watched a TV show.

This thundery evening, with the TV off because of lightning and power surges, I realized my goal of 12 prayer shawls in a year was nearing completion.

My mind swirled with possibilities for the nightly two hours. What should I do next? Teach myself to draw? Get back to practicing the piano? I would need to purchase a keyboard for that. Pursue one of those long-term goals I kept putting off?

Thunder rumbled.

A long-term goal. Had I forgotten writing? No. I had shoved it off to the side, something I wanted but not something I could achieve. That's what I thought. I had given up submitting to the traditional publishers in 2005. What was the point?

Yet I kept writing. Kept coming up with new stories. Inspired by ideas, by characters. Not able to quit creating scenes. Not able to stop finishing manuscripts. Just—not going to submit to the trads or New York agents again. I kept writing until life rolled and rolled and smashed me flat as Gumby.

That night, when I thought about my writing, disgust filled me.

If I just turned off the TV, stopped watching reruns of a TV show that I didn't really care for, I could write for those two hours every evening. I might not have the full two hours Monday through Friday, but I would certainly have additional time on the weekends.

I loved writing, but I couldn't remember when I had last written. Not for years. When?

I immediately put down my crochet and headed for my desk calendar. (By the way, this is an excellent reason to track your writing days.) This was 2012. End of August. And I had written nothing that year. Nothing. Writing for work didn't count.

I turned to the bookshelf where I kept old calendars. 2011. 2010. Nothing. Nothing. 2009? 107 days. Writing a sequel to a story finished in 2007. 2008? Nothing.

Well, I had a reason for not writing anything that year. My mother died following a long mental decay. Grief creates this black hole. You think you're doing well. You're not. It doesn't end. You just get past the black hole and try not to orbit around it.

2007? 149 days. Previous years, around 35% of the year.

I stared at nothing for a while. Then I climbed the stairs to the bonus room where I had an unpacked box (from moving in 2011), a box filled with story ideas. I jerked out the story that I had started in 2009 and carried it down to the couch.

I didn't pick up the crochet again that evening. I re-acquainted myself with that story.

LESSON 5] ACCOMPLISH MORE THAN YOU THINK.

By the end of 2012, in the last four months of the year, I had written for 51 days.

Half of that writing was on weekends. I did have the occasional hour or two in the evenings. I burned through several hours on the weekends when I had no other commitments. Those 51 days are 42% of 122 days in those last four months. Not every other day but coming close. Certainly better than nothing.

I also finished that last prayer shawl.

5A] Every evening that I entered my writing space, I set a timer for two hours.

I can get lost in story. My job needed a brain, so my brain would need its 7 ½ hours of sleep, minimum. I started my evening at 6 and ended at 8.

On those 51 days, I had more staring at the beginning than I liked. I managed a few pages. On bad nights, I wrote only a couple of paragraphs. On a few wondrous evenings, I wrote 10 to 12 pages. I lived for that rushing spate of words.

I didn't have an official goal. Nothing more than finish that book. No plans to submit it or anything else. Just finish.

I didn't finish the book in 2012, but I was happier than I'd been in a long, long, long time, allowing my creative expression to emerge after shutting it down for years.

Here's three more lessons I learned in the tail-end of 2012.

5B] TV is a time suck, just as much as a job is.

TV doesn't give me dollars. Time with the TV is lost, a black hole that I refused to orbit around. It's also a creativity suck. On that fateful August evening—another August decision!—had the TV been on, my brain would not have turned over my world and turned it upside down.

5C] You know what else is a suck? Those phone apps.

Social Media. Phone games. Video games. Browsing on Pinterest. Surfing the Net.

We think it will take only a little bit to check our message stream on the great FB in the cloud. When we look up, two hours have passed. Or we want to finish the game on a high note; there goes 30 more minutes. Pinterest and more are just like looking through catalogs.

5D] So, you've not written in a long while? You can still pick it back up.

It's like riding a bicycle. Or doing crochet. Or playing the piano.

You might stumble a little at the beginning.

Yet the more you write, the more that ideas will flow, and more ideas translate into more words > pages > scenes > chapters > Book!

6TH ~ Invasion of the Story Killers

Lesson 6] Consider your personal Writing Process.

Stories begin with snippets of ideas ~

~ which are then roughed to shape a series of scenes ~

~ that you will draft into a coherent plot of scenes and sequels (Dwight Swain[4] terms) to achieve a complete manuscript ~

~ which will need a bit of revision ~

~ a whole lot of proofreading ~

~ and only then can be prepped for publication, with a blurb and formatting and more.

If you take the traditional route by submitting to an official publishing house, you'll also need a synopsis and outline and query letter and more. If you go the indie route and publish yourself, you'll follow guidelines for uploading to platforms like Amazon, Kobo, iBooks, Ingram Spark, and more. You'll work with a cover designer and maybe a line editor.

6A] Different Stages of Writing Require Different Brains.

The rough shape and draft stages need unbroken creativity and energy. Hour-long stretches of writing are not just desirable but essential.

The idea, revision, proofing, and prepping stages need only attention. Smaller bits of time are acceptable.

When you have 15 spare minutes, you can sketch out ideas, proof, and more. Revising while waiting for appointments, squeezing in corrections while sitting on bleachers, and snatching a couple of pages to sketch are constant possibilities.

The only two actual necessities are your **awareness** of the available bits of time and your **plan** to use them for writing. Doesn't that beat surfing FB or playing a phone game?

The hour-long stretches occur when you decide to use them. Getting up an hour earlier, heading to bed an hour earlier—these are possibilities. Writing two hours every night, that's a definite possibility. Much better than binging on Netflix or vegging-out through another rerun.

The early days of the habit are the most difficult. You have to create reminders.

Reminders that you will SEE. I don't know how many sticky notes I would put on the refrigerator or the microwave, hoping I would *see* them while I was fixing supper, and just totally overlook them.

I stumbled into my greatest help for daily writing.

6B] Privacy and Writing

---

[4] https://www.amazon.com/Techniques-Selling-Writer-Dwight-Swain/dp/0806111917

When I moved into my home in 2011, I had no need of a formal dining space when off the kitchen was a great informal dining area with a large window overlooking the bird feeders. That official formal dining room became my library / home office. Four bookcases for my book collection. The office desk that I bought with eyes bigger than my wallet. For the past few years that desk had become nothing more than a spot to pay bills.

When I resumed writing a year after that move, I naturally headed for the big office desk in the wide-open space right beside my front door.

I hadn't been working many weeks before I had a visitor, one who prowled around the desk, saw printed manuscript pages, and picked them up to read. I didn't even really *know* this woman, and she was reading my story. My un-proofed story. My incomplete story. Oh horror!

- I'm superstitious. When I'm constructing stories, I don't want anyone looking over my shoulder.
    - Maybe that's to keep the story *mine* until it's released into the wild. Maybe it's the old belief that letting someone see the draft will *kill* the story. Whatever, it was an intolerable *invasion*.
- That old belief of killing the story sounds right. I've shared story ideas before. As people commented and criticized and nix-sayed, my little story seedling would shrivel and die.
    - I stopped going to critique groups early on.

On that fateful day when that mere acquaintance of a woman picked up my rough MS pages, I almost cried. I don't know what I expected. I do know that I feared my little story idea would dry up and blow away—and I had just resumed writing! After years of not writing! No. No, no, no! This was not going to happen again.

Once a draft is completed, I can share. The story's out there, with only polishing needed. Not before the completed draft, though.

I don't understand how other writers can use developmental editors. That wouldn't work for me. It's totally okay for them, but my little story seedling or sprout would no longer thrive.

She asked what I was writing. I said a mystery. She put the pages down and joined me in the great room. While we conversed, my brain attacked the problem of keeping a MS private in an open plan house.

6C] Know the Writing Space needs.

Some people can write on the kitchen table. Some people write in bed. I need a flat surface and a chair. I need to be able to put pages on both sides of my flat writing surface.

Some people can write in coffee houses. I wish, for I love an endless supply of coffee. However, the creative muse needs no outside words. Instrumental music encourages the muse; music with words—nope.

Some people need only a laptop. They might have a mouse rather than use the touchpad. Two things, and they're good to go. I need sticky notes and pens, stapler and paper clips, tape and scissors. Paper! Pens! Laptop! Mouse! Laptop!

On that fateful day, when the snooping woman left, I stared at the big office desk of my writing fantasy and declared, "I'm getting real! Time to move my writing space." The printer could stay in the office. The creative writing space would shift to a private area of my house, not a public room.

That meant that it would not be going into a spare bedroom used when family came to visit. How did I solve my problem? And how will you solve yours? Well, that's next.

7ᵗʰ ~ Fertile Spaces for Story Seeds

Lesson 7] Devote a space to writing.

Having a space devoted solely to writing is more than simply having a spot for all of the creative mess to be.

Once using the space becomes habitual, entering it will set off your brain synapses to start creativity. Half of your transition from non-writing to writing is completed simply by walking into your writing space and sitting down at your desk—or opening the laptop on the bed or placing your tablet on a table and clicking away.

When the writing space is located in a private area, you don't risk people messing with your messy-looking organization of the great sprawling mass that is a novel. When it's private, you don't have people poking their noses into a story that you're not ready to release to the world at large.

7A] Locating the space where you will encounter it morning and night helps build the habit of daily writing.

The location creates the reminder.

The reminder drives you into the space.

Entering the space turns on the brain for creativity.

Other Writers' Plots for Sowing Story Seeds

In 2009—which I encountered it three years later (late again!)—*The Guardian* ran a series of special interest columns on the work areas of well-known English writers. "Writers' Rooms," they called it.

My *fantasy* of a writing space was library-like with floor-to-ceiling shelves, filing cabinets as the lower shelf space, two large worktables in addition to a massive desk, and the office equipment hidden behind doors. Also behind doors would be a project board for my Work-In-Progress. A large window with radiant sunshine, birdsong, and a gentle breeze. My work computer and a discrete computer for internet referencing. An assistant—who would need his own office space so his good looks didn't distract me too much. Wall space for my covers as art and for awards and photos with famous people. Oh, and an excellent office chair.

A girl can fantasize, right?

So, the *dream* has snippets of the fantasy but still involves worktables and shelving in addition to a desk, window and ceiling fan, a WIP project board, and place to hide equipment and office supplies. And a great chair. My covers will be the art, in 4 x 6 frames.

The *Guardian* "Writers' Rooms" series set my fantasy back on its high, spiked, cherry pink heels. Many of the writers had only corners in a room. Only a few had devoted spaces. All were creatively messy, with only a couple looking like hoarders. Most of them had started by making-do with a space and just remaining in it because they'd become comfortable with the space and didn't need to change.

After my encounter with *that snoopy woman* (6th Lesson), I devoted a Sunday afternoon to research about writers' spaces. *The Guardian*'s various photos in the series[5] offered tons of ideas. The stories that accompany the photos, writers talking about how their spaces came to be, are as interesting and varied as the spaces themselves are.

7B] That's a key element: your writing space reflects you, not someone else.

You have to decide what you need and where you need it and how you're going to set it up and what eccentric little touches will make it yours.

Tucking Into a Corner

When I moved into my house in 2011, I converted an offset sitting area in the master bedroom—which I didn't need—into a master closet, which was needed. That created a problem, though, for the new master closet was too large for the clothes that I had. I had a corner, about 8 x 6 that stood empty, unused.

No longer. After the invasion of that potential story-killer, my new writing space went into the too-large master closet. A craft table became the flat surface. A task lamp helped the lighting issue. A plastic three-drawer cart held supplies. I used one of the dining chairs as my work chair, not that comfy but not that uncomfortable.

The surface of the craft table felt horrid. I covered it with a pretty scarf then put a clear blotter over it. I had a few little tchotchkes. A nearby window. The ceiling fan in the bedroom provided a gentle breeze.

The space was completely private. Only family would come in, and that would only be when they visited.

The words poured out, which is what matters.

I didn't need a fantasy library/office.

Still want one, though. Working on getting that dream.

Learning the bare basics of what you need to write, that's 7C].

After six years in my house, I moved. Life changes, you know.

Right now my writing space is along a wall in my bedroom. Sometimes I pop out and sit in the family room and draft something non-fiction, like posts for this series.

I'm dreaming of a return to a devoted writing space. With floor-to-ceiling bookcases. A board for the WIP. 4 x 6 photo frames showing my covers.

That little corner in a closet which wasn't really a closet taught a serious lesson :: "Here's the basics needed". When I wrote, my back was to my clothes. I faced the window.

Seeing green, that was all I needed. Oh, and paper and pens.

---

[5] https://www.theguardian.com/books/series/writersrooms

8TH ~ GOING OFF-TRACK

Off-roading can be fun, scary, stressful, and hilarious. Like the famous Jeep commercial suggests, making your own road is better than pancakes.

Of course, not all off-roading ventures are successful.

As writers, we go off-road whenever we don't follow the plan.

LESSON 8] 2 P'S THAT ARE WRITERS

Plotter. Pantster. These are the basic behaviors of all writers. We have variations and combinations. (If you're adding Puzzler, keep reading.) All the diversity actually tracks into one of these two roads.

Plotters outline everything before they begin. They set the Foundation Elements: tagline-plus (theme, direction), character development, story arc, and world building. Then they add an additional setup: they outline or block every scene in the novel.

When everything is planned, then they begin. The writing flies from this point. Revision is minor tweaking.

Pantsters prepare nothing. They launch immediately into story. Character development and story arc happen on the page and maybe get recorded. The world is built as needed. Research stops the flow of writing. Only after the last words are written do they discover the tagline.

The writing ends with a massive revision still to come. Chunks of the story may be tossed. Whole chapters will be re-written or purged completely while new chapters come into the manuscript.

8A] Plotter vs. Pantster

A plotter's life is easy on the back-end because the hard work is at the beginning.

- Plotters zoom along the interstate.
- After working through the city streets, stopping for coffee and donuts, they reach the superhighway, speeding along with all the other vehicles.

A pantster's life is easy on the front with the hard work at the end.

- Pantsters explore off-road. Actually, as explorers of story, they may never find the road.
- They're lured deep into the forest of story as they seek its secret heart.

I've tried both methods.

Forests can be scary. Wild animals and unexpected obstacles can destroy enthusiasm.

Interstates can be boring. We have speeders and big trucks to avoid.

Pantsters are excited as they write. Yet not controlling leaves them with a tangled mess.

Plotters love flying through the difficulty of the draft. However, over-planning can kill enthusiasm for the story.

A mix of the two styles is the best and shunts aside most problems. Keeping an open mind about both styles is my current struggle: Foundational planning without scene blocking, rough writing while keeping my tagline and story arc clear.

8B] Enter the Puzzler.

Two definitions of Puzzler are floating around, one that sounds like a writing style and the other that sounds like a drafting process. (The drafting process is 8C. Promise.)

The first definition of Puzzler is to launch into story, filling in the Foundational elements as needed and working through the problems like box canyons and detours for construction. This combines Pantster and Plotter worlds.

The second definition of Puzzler is to write a scene here and there and over yonder. That scene will fit into a specific stage of the story arc, which the writer is well aware of. Then the Puzzler writes another scene from a different part of the story arc. Gradually, the puzzle pieces of story are filled in, just like a jigsaw puzzle: border, clouds, green expanse, flower garden left and right, castle in the middle, extra little areas.

Writing the Puzzler style is like driving through the city and encountering traffic so you hop off and detour through a nearby national park, then you jump back onto the interstate until you reach one of the exits you can use, picking the one that's a meander along backroads to avoid more traffic until you find the secondary road that leads to your main road which you then bullet-fly to home.

8C] Drafting Story

The basic distinction of plotter vs. pantster vs. puzzler is not from the drafting process.

We really only have two Drafting Processes.

- Chronological or Linear
- Global or Scattered

The Global/Scattered is the second definition of the Puzzler. The writer constructs the manuscript by writing scenes in no particular order: cute meet, climax, obstacle 3, intro 1, resolution, angst 2, and so on. Enthusiasm for the story remains elevated at the beginning for the more interesting scenes are written first. Then the writer's enthusiasm begins a steady decline. First , the sequels (or bridges) between the interesting scenes are constructed. The writer drags through the most difficult scenes and their bridges.

Whether writing beginning to end or vice versa, the straight-line Chronological approach is closest to the reader / audience experience. Difficult scenes are dealt with as they occur. The interesting scenes fly. The writer's enthusiasm level is a roller coaster. By mimicking the reader's experience, the writer can more easily spot when the writing creates muck and can then ramp up interest by using more action or humor or emotional attachments.

So ~

- Do you want to drive off-road? Sounds exciting. Beware of pitfalls.
- Or would you rather drive the interstate? Speeding along, all breezy. Until a traffic accident causes a huge back-up.
- Or do you mix it up, combining all types of driving.

The glory is that you can change your writing behavior and your drafting process at will.

You can Plot 10 Scattered scenes, then Pants the bridge sequels, Pants more scenes in a Chronological fired frenzy of writing, then Pants & Scatter followed by Plot and Chrono.

8D] You can do anything you want. Just be aware of what you're doing.

When you get stuck, switch it around.

No writer is one or the other or the third. Writing is a spectrum that we slide along, changing and adapting with every writing session.

Trying new and different techniques is fun. Sometimes, our best intentions lead us into pitfalls, whether we're on the main road or off-roading.

Next is a bit about the analytical techniques I use even though my personality cringes at the thought. Read on for "Ticky Boxes."

9ᵀᴴ ~ Ticky Boxes

Analytical personalities love plans. They love charts. They love filling in little boxes and squares.

Filling in little boxes doesn't make me happy.

Unless it does.

Sounds contradictory, doesn't it? My personality is a little contradictory as well.

See, sometimes I think I'm a closet analytical personality. Tracking my progress through writing projects pleases me and keeps me focused on completing those projects.

Now, I do know the reason for this. If I don't know where I am in the project, if it looks like it will go on *ad finitum*, then I will abandon it.

Learning that I need to track progress is one of those biggie self-analysis surprises. I don't do well with most authority figures. Point out a law, and I'm usually looking for a way around it. Tell me that something has to be done this way means that I will find a way to nudge a toe across the line.

Charts help us visualize how much of a project remains. I'm good with creating my own charts and filling them in with pretty colors. That's contentment. Make me fill out a chart that I didn't design or tinker with, however, *oh boy*. Is that a thundercloud coming?

Trackers and charts come too close to exact planning. I'm not really good with imposed planning. I'm happy to create my own schedule. My former work required a week's plan in advance. After turning in the plan on Friday afternoon, I would be off-track by Tuesday. That happened because I over-planned each day.

Over-planning meant that Monday had to flow into Tuesday which streamed on to Thursday while Friday became next Wednesday. It's a bit of subversive rebellion. "See, I'm planning. I planned too well. We're off schedule on the plan because we're behind. This is where we're going."

I defy any authority figure to tell me that's the wrong way to plan.

Lesson 9] For novels, over-planning is problematic.

A little planning is necessary: tagline, character development, story arc. Blocking out each scene, following the Beats with page percentages, outlining specific conflicts and events and motifs, that ruins a story for me. As I write, I expect the same entertainment that I want as a reader.

Planning means knowing the story ahead of time. Reveal too much, and curiosity flies away.

That happened last year. I started a novel in late April. I spent hours blocking out every scene: conflict, actions, snippets of dialogue, motifs that I usually reserve for the revision stage.

By 1ˢᵗ May, just as planned, I was ready to start writing. All through May, June, and July I struggled with that book. I wrote a scene, didn't think it worked, so I re-wrote it from another character's viewpoint. Over 90 days, and I found myself hunting up other projects rather than that one. Every writing session dragged. Even as I saw the story shaping, I knew I wasn't achieving the story I had imagined before I began all the scene blocking.

Ninety days. Few of those spent on this novel project. Not quite 10,000 words achieved. Going nowhere fast.

I tried to jumpstart the story in August with an online course on Depth from Dean Wesley Smith. That course was a wonderful help. It inspired me. I started changing the quality of the words I was writing for the course. I jumped back to the beginning of my novel and applied the lessons. As I did so, a secondary character demanded to become a primary character. Once I gave him a voice, the novel took off. I wrote more during the last week of July and first two weeks of August than I had written in the previous 12 weeks.

In August, I also attended a writers' conference. Killer Nashville is the best little conference that few people know about. I didn't know anyone, so I spent the evenings writing scenes for the new character voice and continuing ahead. I had left my blocked scenes at home, and I was "forced" to write fresh :: Best thing that happened all conference. So, Killer Nashville served a two-fold purpose for me as both a conference and a retreat.

The dam was broken. When I returned home, I continued with the new scenes. At the end of every writing session, I jotted a list of the ideas swirling. At the start of the next session, I read that list, jotted a new one, and began writing. At the end of each week, I checked the old abandoned blocked scenes. Gradually, over the next four months, I tore up the abandoned plan, ventured into completely new scenes, and didn't worry because the story constructed itself naturally.

By early January, I had close to 98,000 finished words.

9A] Shake-up the routine.

If you're a veteran writer, you might need a shake-up just like this one.

If you're a newbie, do NOT do this. You need guidance. Not a lot and certainly not the over-planning that so many advise. The novel's Foundation needs to be set, and you need an abbreviated idea of the story arc.

9B] Know when you can abandon the plan.

I knew I could safely abandon my previous planning for these two reasons:

- I have long experience—in analysis and application—of story structure, specifically the Archetypal Story Pattern. I also know the flow and pacing necessary for the story arc and character development. I had a tagline (theme) that served as my touchstone for every newly-written scene. Any event that didn't fit the tagline wasn't written.
- The bones of the story, the Foundation, never abandon those: Character specifics, dynamics, and angst. Primary conflict. Secondary conflict. World-building and research for that world of Spain in 1814. These Foundation elements of the story remained untouched.

9C] The Foundation has to be pre-set.

Doing research instead of writing a scene will offend your creative muse.

Set the Foundational roots of your tree. Those roots may never appear on the manuscript page, but they have to be solid before the trunk of your story can grow, strengthen, and create branches which will leaf.

10TH ~ CLIMBING OUT OF THE BOX

Keeping word counts and tracking project progress from Foundation to Rough Shape to Draft to Proof-Plus is not following straight lines. These help you see progress.

LESSON 10] SEEING PROGRESS KEEPS US PROGRESSING.

Word counts and progress meters take only a bare minute to record.

In Lesson 9, I revealed my difficulties with over-planning a novel. Even though I was on the planned interstate of plotting details and dialogue for every scene, I ran into a major pitfall. I lost all curiosity about my story. I knew every detail.

I need the reader experience as I write. By over-planning, I lost my desire to discover the story that is *The Key for Spies* (my M.A. Lee pseudonym).

I had thought that I would make my life simpler by doing what so many writers were advocating. Instead, I derailed my muse. She harassed me about making the story better—but that wasn't following my plan. When I tried to ignore that impish muse, the story went nowhere.

- I gradually added more words to the story, but I was far off my usual pace.
- Avoidance took over. I sought out two other major projects along with every distracting activity. Those projects kept me accomplishing, but not on the primary project.
- Self-doubt, now called Imposter Syndrome, kept asking if I was truly a writer.

How did I discover what had derailed my writing? I mean, with all the distractions and busy work, how did I realize what was happening.

10A] Word counts and progress checks. Those Ticky Little Boxes.

At the end of May, I totaled up the word counts for *The Key for Spies* and major busy-work project #1. "Wow," I thought. "Not really getting much done. I'm supposed to finish that book before August. So, 60 days left. I should be able to finish."

June ended. Again, I totaled up word counts. Side project #1 was now complete. I had started a second side project. And added barely 5,000 words on *K4Spies*. Ouch. That's when I realized the novel had derailed.

July came. And went. Nowhere close to 5,000 words. As I noted previously, my total word count for the project, after 90 days, was less than 10,000 words.

The second side project neared completion.

I know my word counts for *The Key for Spies* because my word counts are recorded daily / weekly / monthly / yearly. I know that June lumbered along while September and October took flight before the disruptions of November. Tracking word counts and keeping project progress with daily counts helps me *see* that I'm achieving.

A couple of years ago, when I looked for a word count tracker, I did find an MS Excel chart online. It worked. Automatically updated once I filled in the numbers. I didn't like it. The segments are not lined up the way I want them to be. I can't do pretty colors.

This year was the discovery of a progress meter for my website. The progress meter displays the percentage completed based on my projected word count. The novel's cover and the tagline go with the progress meter. I do like this handy add-on.

Updates to the progress meter happen once a month when I'm not distracted. More than that, though, creates its own distraction.

10B] Whatever you find, it should work for you.

Just filling in numbers is not enough. You should have satisfaction in seeing the numbers grow and the progress being checked off.

11ᵗʰ ~ Don't Hate Numbers and Lists

Writers need to track each writing session and show the accumulating progress. It's too hard to focus on what we're not getting accomplished. Last year, after the morass of May and June and July, feeling that nothing was going well, I listed everything that I had accomplished in my writing biz so far. By highlighting accomplishments specifically for 2018, I saw my successes.

That list helped me overcome self-doubt. "Imposter Syndrome, take that! Pow!"

Lesson 11] Keep an Accomplishments List

Too easily we dwell on failures when we should celebrate successes. Each time we complete a part of a project, we need a mini celebration, and we need to give ourselves a huge celebration when we finish a massive project like a novel, with its hidden roots and its sturdy trunk and its many-branched limbs covered with wonderful word leaves.

When self-doubt assails us, we can look at our tracks, our accomplishments list, and our celebrations large and small. All are proof that we're not in fantasy; we're in a new reality. A rockslide tried to wipe us out, but we're still going.

My struggles with *The Key for Spies* didn't signal a failure. I was growing as a writer, learning more about my craft and discovering the road back to listen to an intuitive sense of story. The Accomplishments List removed the blinders caused by the failures. Watching the words pour out after I listened to the intuitive muse helped.

11A] Quantifying can distract us.

When our purpose becomes counting words, pages, and chapters, we're not considering the quality of our writing. We can turn progress meters and daily word counts and writing sprints with our Pomodoro timers into the whole focus and forget the most important thing.

All writing needs a focus on ideas, themes, and images to emphasize those ideas.

Just because we need to record word counts and track our progress does not mean that we lose our focus on story.

11B] Blocks do offer opportunities, not slogging into muck.

That monumental struggle with *Key4Spies* drove me to pursue two side projects that I had procrastinated over. When the novel refused to go, I set it aside to give the impish muse time to work.

In those 90 struggling days, the side projects worked to their conclusion. One of them gave a planner for writers—which I now use for tracking my word counts and project progress. The other side project was a planner for the health-conscious, a planner that reminds us that health is more than physical—it's also emotional and mental and spiritual.

I also completed the Great Website Rebuild. I wanted to have Pillar Pages with links. The Writers Ink Books website devotes a page to each pseudonym. Even stripped down, the pages are jammed with images and book trailers and buy links. The Writers Ink Services website for nonfiction does look stripped-down, with true pillar pages. I'll rebuild that site soon, with a new domain name, pillar pages, and focused purpose.

So, from late May to the end of August, I completed two planners and a website re-build, took an online course, and planned to go to a writing conference. Not what I had planned, but what would be profitable for my time. Over those months, the muse danced around, for as soon as I completed those five projects, *K4Spies* started pouring out.

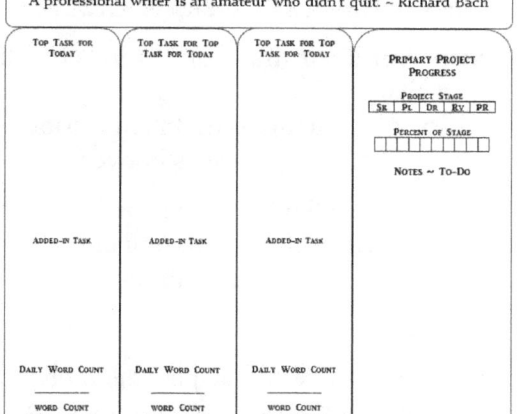

I didn't plow ahead, churning out words to create chapters that would have to be gutted. I zigged away. All because I remembered the most important thing. Do you remember it? It's the goal.

We want to *make a living writing interesting books*.

When the story becomes words plugged onto a page, when our curiosity is quenched by over-planning, when we're no longer entertained by our own stories, we have distracted ourselves from the goal.

Over-planning is one story killer.

Not planning is another.

If you fear plowing into the ground, keep a side project going.

Continue on for the problems of Saggy Pantstering.

12TH ~ SAGGY PANTSTERING & CREATIVITY

New writers craft their first 4 or 5 stories by mimicking their reader experience: opening the story, following a character from the beginning to end of the conflict, and closing with a good feeling. As they work to complete these first manuscripts, they devote their energies to the exciting scenes and skip the boring parts (the bridges between).

When Newbies take the Wannabee path, they model their writing on films and stories that they liked. They fill pages with descriptions and actions and dialogue based on other writers' characters and stories. It's fan fiction, whether they share it or keep it to themselves.

Modeling *is* a tried-and-true method for new writers to improve their skills. It does work.

Some Wannabees never move past the modeling stage. They're content with fan fiction. And that's their choice. We can do what we want with our own writing. No one is dictating to us. Our path is our own, no one else's. If someone tries to tell you what to do with your writing, tell them where to get off your train.

Modeling is a learning step. Learning how other professionals craft their characters and plots and exposition details is a crucial step. Modeling, however, only takes a writer part-way.

The important step after modeling, the one that Gonnabee writers have to learn, is this: Generating Original Ideas.

LESSON 12] GROWTH DEPENDS ON ACCEPTING CHALLENGES.

12A] The first challenge is improving your writing.

12B] The second challenge is reading widely to learn from the masters.

12C] The third challenge is stepping beyond the model to tell your own story.

Creating your own world, peopling it, and driving those characters through a conflict, that's a rewarding challenge.

Now, in the millennia since story-telling began, around the campfire tales after the day's hunt to the coffee shop discussions about artificial electronic books, we really have nothing new to learn, just new twists on classic stories.

Even non-linear plot, like Quentin Tarantino's *Pulp Fiction* is an innovation on the style Homer used in *The Iliad*.

New characters are spins on archetypes. New story lines fit into one of the 7 types of plots. The progress of the plot follows a handful of structures. Creativity comes NOT with these.

12D] Creativity comes in unique spins on the classic.

Creative growth is accepting the challenge to innovate with the classic characters and plots, themes and motifs, drives and urges and angst. Innovation and elaboration: these *create* a new-ness of story.

Look at J.K. Rowlings' Harry Potter series. Analyze any part of the series. As a longtime eclectic reader, you quickly discover that she mined mythologies and archetypal events and details. Her combination of these with an orphaned Chosen One protagonist encountering engaging allies, juxtaposed mentors, and challenging antagonists (physical, mental, and emotional ones) created the new-ness.

Her writing communicated the story easily. Accessibility *is* the key to reaching a large marketplace. Great marketing did the rest.

None of J.K. Rowling's "details" are *new*. Her creativity is in her combination, communication, and appeal.

If the story's not new and characters aren't new and the situations aren't new (only the newest tech is new until it's obsolete), then what is *new*?

That answer is coming up.

13th ~ Creativity leads to Saggy Pantstering

Creativity is new-ness. Actually, *new* is the wrong word.

Lesson 13] Creativity is freshness.

Merriam-Webster (my go-to dictionary) failed me. Its definition of creativity is *the ability to create*. Merriam-Webster's Thesaurus says *the skill and imagination to create new things*. Alrighty, then. Those aren't helpful.

Let's try Dictionary.com ~

Creativity ~ The ability to transcend traditional ideas, rules, patterns, relationships or the like, and to create new ideas, forms, methods, interpretations, etc.; originality, progressiveness, or imagination.

In practice, creativity is three things:

13A] invention of something completely new.

A completely new invention is rare.

13B] combination of several known (traditional) elements into an unexpected new.

This is innovation. (à la J.K. Rowling and Quentin Tarantino).

13C] Elaboration of details of the known (traditional) in unusual ways.

Elaboration is ornamentation.

So, what does this have to do with Pantstering and not planning?

Unless you as the writer spend time mulling over how to freshen your story, how to twist the known into a new combination, how to bring something new onto the page, then the common / traditional forms of characters, plot, situation, and more will be mere repetition of ancient patterns.

That's the downfall of pantstering. You can write a story without a plan, develop characters on the fly and build situations and worlds from scratch. That's not hard.

Adding creativity? Ouch.

Creativity / freshness requires thought.

Pantsters claim they don't plan so the creative muse can speak to them. And that's true. Over-plotting can kill a story. Creativity, however, is not plan-less.

Creatives have to plan. They look at what's needed then start cogitating, twisting ideas around, developing new.

Spend hours, days, longer considering your new invention / combination / elaboration. You need not write them down. Any thought that you put into your consideration, recorded or not, is still planning. You may dictate, create a board with images, keep the whole story in your head ~ you're still planning.

And that's Saggy Pantstering.

You've got ideas. Form doesn't matter ~ list, images, sketch, words. You're planning. You avoid outlines and anything that looks "official". The unofficial—still planning.

Saggy Pantstering is a successful form of writing. Revision will be necessary. The uncontrolled mess that is pure pantstering, however, you have avoided.

Pure Pantstering throws everything in. The protagonist changes. The antagonist changes. Several scenes may have 3 or 6 or 10 versions. More scenes may be unrelated. No tagline / theme focuses the story.

Along the writing journey, writers can fall into the rabbit hole of Pure Pantstering. They won't find themselves in Wonderland. Nope. They're in a warren, with a mad prophet screaming riddles they don't understand and bunnies hopping off in every direction, the leader lost or non-existent.

Escape the warren. Do a little planning before you launch into story.

Invent something new.

Combine the traditional into a new innovation.

Elaborate in unusual ways.

Give the old a fresh spin ~ as Richard Adams did with *Watership Down*.

The practice of creativity leads to more creativity. Creative thoughts breed like bunnies. You can drop them into Wonderland or the warren.

Stories are the result.

Next up is a step back: the Zig and Zag of Handling Long-Term Projects

14TH ~ ZIG AND ZAG

Writing behavior determines our approach to the mass of story: roots, trunk, branches, leaves. We can plot or "pants" (a woefully inadequate word, but someone wanted the alliterative P, and it stuck.) or puzzle it out.

As you draft your manuscript, you can use a chronological / linear process or be scattered / global.

Tracking daily word counts and project progress helps overcome the intimidating writing discipline as well as imposter syndrome.

Discipline is the third thing that writers need to understand about themselves.

LESSON 14] THE DAILY HABIT OF WRITING IS EASILY BROKEN.

Writers battle disruptions and distractions. Procrastination whispers that we can resume it, "later".

Choosing to become a writer who writes daily—having a steadily climbing word count that will finish projects—means that we encounter days when the writing is more coercion than choice.

Let's admit that, upfront, immediately. Writing can be drudgery rather than fiery inspiration. All of the words of the scenes and the sequels (Dwight Swain terms) must be completed to finish the manuscript. Every story has cringe-worthy moments. Readers can skim or skip those; writers slave through every word. And once we know the end of the story, we want to move to the next shiny, bright thing.

Daily, hourly, we are lured away.

With those of us writing on the side, other people and work and stress and chores and errands and weariness and *sweariness* and needed exercise will break the daily commitment. Skip a day or two or three, and soon we've skipped an entire week. *How does that happen?* we ask, and then it happens the next week and the next.

The daily habit rapidly falls apart, melting links in a chain we thought was strong iron but actually was merely hard-frozen glacier ice. Add heat, add neglect, and the links dissolve.

14A] Commitment helps overcome the lures.

We have to climb back into our writing chairs and write the first sentence then the next and the third and the fourth, on to the completion of a paragraph, a page, a scene, a chapter.

When we don't write the next sentence and the next then the next, we start looking for something to blame.

Some writers blame Writer's Block. "It's haunting me," they cry.

I'm going to offend many writers here :: Writer's Block doesn't exist. Fact! Research all the professionals who support this statement.

Want to escape any block? Put Bum in Chair and write a sentence and the next then the next.

We can write. We can text, send emails, post on social media. That's writing, folks. We may not feel like it. We may have lost interest in the story we need to tell. We're not blocked, however.

In my first guidebook for writers, *Think like a Pro*, (under my pseudonym of M.A. Lee) I devote an entire chapter to the fallback claim of Writer's Block. That problem is actually one of three:

- Writer's Refusal ~ We don't want to do what we should be doing.
- Writer's Procrastination ~ This stifling obstacle is born in fear, of failure or of judgment.
- Writer's Inertia ~ boredom or depression and stagnation. Inertia can be a true monster.

In *Think like a Pro* are several methods to diagnose the problem as well as the solutions to overcome it.

14B] Zig Off to a New Project

One way to prevent the drudgery that drives us out of our writing chair is to zig off to another project. I mentioned this solution in the post for the 11th.

Having an alternate project maintains the daily writing. It gives a break (or two or three) when the creative muse needs to work behind the scenes.

Whenever you cast away from the primary project, you risk dropping it entirely. The key to a Zig Off is to return to the primary when the bright, shiny new has served its purpose.

Remember, as long as you are producing, no time is ever wasted.

Novels and long-term projects have many stages. We move from sketched ideas to shaped scenes, on to the drafted manuscript which we then revise and proof before prepping for publishing. Each of those stages requires different skills.

In ideas, we develop situations, characters, tagline/themes, plot stream, and world-building. We then shape the plot stream, building each up to fulfill our vision of the story arc. The draft is the long slog, the most enjoyable yet frustrating part of the story. We reach 23 chapters of a 35-chapter novel, and we want to abandon the whole thing.

When that 24th chapter is driving you mad, you can always zig off to work on your blurb, also called market copy or back-cover copy. You can refine the tagline, which can turn into an all-day slog with less than 20 words when you're finished. You can sketch ideas for the next project.

14C] Remember to Zag Back to the Primary Project.

Remember not to churn out words on the primary project. Writing into the muck will weaken the creative muse. Consider the overall plan and the last session's jot list. Keep everything fresh. Take breaks, especially if you need to break from a project—then zag back and pick up where you left off.

Remind yourself of the incremental achievement of each stage by using progress meters. Celebrate each stage's completion. The major celebration, fireworks and all, occurs when you launch the book into the world, whether that is self-publishing or sending to an editor or an agent.

Daily words are also incremental achievements. When you have a weekly word count to achieve and to celebrate, then your sense of accomplishment helps you overcome the drudgery and helps you defeat the seductive lures that entice you away from your writing chair.

The word count itself is a zig-zag plan. Once you're writing regularly, you know how many words you can achieve reasonably.

- Multiply that daily average by 5 (or 6, with only one day off for creative re-charging) for the weekly word count. This is the zig.
- The zag happens when interruptions occur—and they will, no matter what you plan.
- When I don't achieve my base word count on Tuesday, I work harder until I've caught up.
- When the whole week is destroyed, don't burden the lost words by throwing the missing word count into the next week. That just carries failure with you. Avoid that baggage, and start the next week with the original word count.
- Glory days occur. When I go over my word count, those are bonus words. Enjoy them. Don't apply them backwards or forwards. They can count to help a destroyed day within a week. Past / future calculations don't come into play.

Zigging and zagging help cross the minefield with its snarls of barb-wire obstacles, underground disruptions exploding around you, and mucky drudgery that you have to crawl through.

Be a good writing soldier. Maintain your daily discipline. Progress through projects. Switch up your drafting process when you encounter walls. Be willing to transform your writing behavior and achieve your goal ~ of writing interesting books!

15TH ~ EVER-EXPANDING

One of the essentials when you want to be a Daily Writer of Stories is to keep moving, adapting, dancing. Disruptions and distractions are easy to blame and shrug off. Losing track of daily writing is another; you don't want to break that habit.

LESSON 15] WHAT DO WE DO, THOUGH, WHEN THE STORY IS EVER-EXPANDING?

What does *ever-expanding* mean? Here are the symptoms ~ The writing is going great. You love everything, but—characters and events keep inserting themselves into the story. You planned 25 chapters, and you've blown past to reach 30 with more to come. You're 15,000 words and counting over your projected word count.

And everything planned after this story is now thrown off-schedule by the ever-expanding current story.

You don't want to cut the book prematurely. Great things are happening. The muse is dancing, not dashing away. All the scenes are connected and depend upon each other. Devious twists are occurring. What to do?

15A] Actually, there's not really a lot that you can do. Just keep drafting and typing and working for the end.

That book might turn into a two-parter or a prequel with the actual original planned book. When everything's connected, however, you can't really divide things out. (At least, I don't like to read divided-up stories. I'm not much for cliff-hangers, and I'm really unhappy when I realize that the book I'm seven chapters into actually started in a previous book.)

Reader experience is a key element of the decision of whether to divide the story.

In my pseudo of M.A. Lee, I'm working to finish a book that should have come out in June. Forty-five days ago. That's a wow. Deadline completely blown. If I were in traditional publishing, this would be a HUGE problem. I'm self-published; I can let the creative muse play.

15B] Does blowing my deadline mean that I'm a failure?

No. Heavens, no! All it means is that the story took hold and demanded much more than I originally planned. I'm really happy with this novel.

A schedule only helps us look forward to the next bright shiny. (That's an important writing tip!) In my previous existence, I lived for weekends and holidays. Now, every day seems like the weekend and a holiday!

I don't need a zig and zag. Words are pouring out. And *The Hazard of Secrets*, by my pseudonym M.A. Lee, is expanding more and more. First, the Cute Meet trope turned into dangerous events with a press gang, human trafficking, and street urchins. Then, the murder mystery turned into a murder plus a double attempted murder plus a contemplated murder followed by a second actual murder. And none of those are connected to the poisoning!

Originally, the novel was going to be 50,000 words. Then the press gang took over. The street urchins became snippy little allies.

I backed up the publication date to July 15 then July 30 then August 15. It didn't make that publication date. The story kept plugging along. I remained happy with it. The impish muse kept dancing around a tree, throwing falling fruit almost faster than I could catch it. I did my job while I tried to avoid distractions—and Summer is full of distractions!

As for those 50,000 words ~

I hit the mark of 50,000 words when I started typing chapter 16 on July 26. The rough draft was in chapter 23 at that point, with a best guess-timate of 58,000 words for the word count. (I distinguish between my rough draft and my typing draft, the second much more cleaned-up than the first.)

I typed to 60,000 words on August 6. On Saturday August 10, I closed off the laptop at 68,817 words and chapter 20. Mid-August I was drafting chapter 27 with more still to come.

The book topped out at close to 110,000 words with 30-plus chapters. Finishing the last chapter didn't finish my work. I still had proof-plus before publishing. *The Hazard of Secrets* reached twice the expected length. Publication occurred on September 2.

The ever-expanding novel also happened the previous year with *The Key for Spies*, at over 95,000 words, 30,000 more than planned.

As a writer, am I scared about my schedule and the time taken up by *The Hazard of Secrets*? And *The Key for Spies*? Nope. I relished each revealed scene, especially with the additions from that impish muse.

And that's what matters.

16TH ~ SOUL-SUCKING JOBS

Halfway through, and we finally reach the outside influencers on our writing time and energies.

Every writer dreams of quitting the day job and writing full-time.

Some people aren't suited for the self-discipline needed to write full-time. Only a few can handle time uncontrolled by outside forces. Most of us have to wait until retirement to pursue our dream of writing fulltime.

I started early with the dream of *making a living writing interesting stories.* As I approached my work-world years, I actively searched for the ideal career to train myself to become a writer. I considered working in journalism. Or marketing and advertising. Or teaching English.

As the fallback job—because who begins the dream expecting *not* to succeed?—I picked English. I thought learning about literature and composition would give me the necessary background for writing. I did learn the hard skills for writing (Hard Skills = the specific, teachable skills needed to succeed at any job). When my completed manuscript didn't sell, I had to take a money-making job.

LESSON 16] JOBS THAT PAY THE BILLS ARE ESSENTIAL.

I tried journalism. Actually, I fell into a job at the local newspaper as a copy writer.

Weekly deadlines kept me in constant rotation with each day's necessities. The managing editor was kind enough to allow me a weekly column and sent me out on various writing assignments: business articles, a few advertising articles disguised as business, a few human-interest filler pieces, that kind of thing. Mostly, though, I turned out copy on the local sewing circles and garden clubs and more.

Didn't pay very much at all. As a matter of fact, having received a couple of teeny-tiny raises (one-tenth of one percent) and working 50-plus hours each week, my take-home pay was below the poverty line. I was *only* a copy writer, not a reporter.

I left that job and nearly doubled my income by becoming a high school English teacher. *Now*, I thought, *I'll really be learning about writing stories*. Nyah. Not so. Analyzing stories, yes. Grading countless essays that all said virtually the same thing, yep, that's exactly what I was doing.

Sanity demanded that I creatively twist common essay topics: "Instead of writing about Friendship, let's write about The Perfect Enemy." Kept them interested. Kept me from pulling my hair out. A side benefit was learning more about grammar, usage, and mechanics than I needed for writing stories, but hey. Pay was good. Perks like health insurance and a pension were better.

The newspaper job and the teaching job had one thing in common: they absolutely sucked up all the writing energy I had. My creative muse exhausted herself, first with trying to turn window-tint for cars into something interesting and then with trying to create interesting lesson plans for teenagers.

Now, decades on from my own teen years and thinking about careers for writers, I'm not certain there is an ideal career to prepare anyone to be a writer.

16A] Best Training for a Writer

Remember WIBBOW? Would I be better off writing?

The same question you ask yourself for deciding how to spend your writing efforts is the same question that you have to answer for your writing career.

While you may want the answer to be *yes, Yes, YES!*, the correct answer may be *No, not now*.

Most writers, true in the past and the present, never make a living at writing. It's a side job. Every generation a few do make a living. They may not achieve best-seller status. You may never have heard of them. They write tens of thousands of words every month. These lucky few treat writing like their main job and live off their earnings.

Because it's a side job, the time you have for writing does have to use the WIBBOW question.

You have bills to pay? Gotta have the soul-sucking job to pay them. You can still find time to write.

You have to manage your time carefully. You won't be hitting the word counts that you want; you'll have to season the wish with reality. You don't have to give up the dream while reality crowds into every corner of life.

Budget your time and your money, and you can pay for covers as well as that vacation for the family.

Because you're writing more slowly, you will have time to think about the story while you're away from the writing. You can figure out the next scenes that you need to write before you approach your writing space. No staring at the empty page wondering what's next.

16B] The only problem arises when the day job sucks all your creative energies.

The jobs that do pay well are creativity vampires. They actively suck creative blood from your veins and continue sucking until you are the walking dead. These jobs are so demanding that you never even notice everything you've lost. Eventually, though, you do find a way to carve separation: this much for the job, this much for the writing.

So, you think, *I'll take one of the other jobs. You know, the ones that don't suck up all my creativity.* Unfortunately, those jobs don't pay well. The boredom can kill your interest and curiosity. When those die, creativity will shrink and shrivel into a dried husk. The lack of money creates additional stresses that carry far beyond just meeting your bills. Try *no vacation*. Try *worrying about car repairs*. Try *the rent going up while your boss cuts the number of hours that you work*.

Writing full-time is one of those jobs that doesn't pay well. Unless you achieve best-seller status and then *license* your ideas to films and video gaming and toys and more.

You decide, and live with your decision. The balance between the extremes is difficult to find and to manage when you're only considering yourself.

In the poker game where Family, Career, and Writing have placed their bets, Writing will fold pretty quickly.

- Find your balance.
- Live with your decision.
- Meet your obligations.
- Carve out the time you need for writing.

These are the only requirements.

17TH ~ More Soul-Sucking

Writing can be wonderful. When the words are flowing, the story is coming together, and the deadline is achievable, everything is bright and beautiful.

When the writing's not going well, a writer obsesses. Even as we go about our day jobs, deal with family and friends, attend to our various obligations, the story is sucking on us, draining all our attention.

New ideas grab our focus. Stories get started—and then it takes a while to realize the story ran off the trail into a ridge with the deep, dark virgin forest towering overhead and blocking all views of the sky. We hack a way through tangling scenes and encounter scary characters who wielded their own machetes to our original story idea.

When we emerge from the forest, with cell phone service giving the appearance of safety, we think we're back on the right track and continue on.

Maybe we are. Maybe we aren't. Sometimes we don't discover *which* until we reach the end of the story.

Another way that writing becomes soul-sucking is in the race to produce more books—rather than tell more stories. We are desperate to publish more and faster, and the rat on the treadmill keeps spinning in our heads. We take courses about marketing our books and buying advertising on various platforms when we would be better off writing.

Lesson 17] Story is always our main focus.

Our #1 job is to write. More content, more stories, more poems, more whatever it is that we are writing. This is what builds our name, our backlist, our brand, our readership.

Marketing happens only when we have a backlist that will support the newest book. Worry about the marketing when you have a double handful of books. Until then, worry about the next story.

Too many writers finish one manuscript and want to throw everything behind that. Nope. Worry about the next story.

Too many writers think the answer is quick production. Nope. Telling a good story is the answer. Don't look at what other people are doing. Look at what you can do.

17A] Soul-Sucking People can interfere with our stories.

Toxic people in our close circle are hard to avoid. We have to find ways around them. My family once had a toxic person who disrupted countless family gatherings—until we learned that she wouldn't cause a disruption if our gatherings were at restaurants. *Voila!* Solution found.

Sometimes the soul-sucker can be defeated that easily—although it took us more than a handful of years to figure out that solution.

The toxic people at home and work are constant irritations, but we'll eventually find ways to remove them from our lives.

Unexpected toxicity occurs in the writing community. A member of a critique group who enjoys acid criticism too much. A fellow writer who spends more time disparaging professionals. Ivory Tower people who look down their noses at the lesser mortals. These are expected toxic people.

It's the occasional encounters of people who scorn your whole focus that can throw you into an unexpected loop.

The next time you attend a writer's conference or a single-day seminar, look around at your fellow attendees.

Chances are the majority are retirees, the curmudgeonly souls who survived the daily grind and are intent on pursuing the writing dreams delayed for decades. Many are total newbies driven by the dream. A few have tinkered along the way yet still ask newbie questions. With sucking jobs finished and living the writing dream, they're more willing to try new things.

- Talk to them about self-publishing, though, and they shake their heads. That's too different from their long-term dream of book tours, articles in writing magazines, a sinecure at a university as the professional writer on staff.

On the fringe are the bright souls who think they will sell lots and live well. They come in various flavors, mostly cheery pink. They have started a lot of stories with interesting premises; they can't decide which manuscript to finish. They're looking for someone to give them the help necessary to push their book to the top. Developmental editor? Content editor? Yes! No matter how much they cost. Their enthusiasm is contagious.

- Talk to them about self-publishing, though, and they shake their heads. Traditional publishing is the way to go. All they need is an agent and an editor, and best-seller status is *assured*.

The few in the middle had idealistic friends. Those friends have dropped out of writing; it didn't become profitable quickly enough. These middle few remain, writing because they can't stop. They are truly story tellers. They just need the extra oomph to get into publishing.

- Talk to them about self-publishing, though, and they shake their heads. Once they walk away, they sneer that the indie writer is just a vanity writer.

No matter which writer you want to be, traditionally published or indie all the way or a hybrid of the two, you need to deal with the newbies and Wannabees and Gonnabees and everyone else with kindness. The path they're taking may not be your path. It doesn't have to be your path. You can go your own way.

17B] The only people that you don't have to be nice to are the shysters.

The publishing industry is crawling with these ticks. These are the people who promise a manuscript edit for major bucks that will guarantee your book becomes a best-seller.

Or they're the unscrupulous agents who bilk their clients of millions (like the agency for the *Fight Club* writer).

Or they promote their small press, and they do publish your manuscript while also selling it on to cheap sites (breaking copyright laws in the process and hoping you never track the trail).

The shyster writers chatter about the newest scam: click-farms, book stuffing, buying reviews, or using desperate work-for-hire writers and calling them their ghostwriters.[6]

Then we have the shyster writers touting the best method. They offer it in an online seminar ~ Sign up for $759.99. It's hard to distinguish these sludgy mucks from the good guys. Your key is their publishing history. If you can't find their books, don't trust their course offerings. The good guys are out there; you just have to find them.

With so many soul-sucking shysters in the writing biz, it's a wonder that the rosy-colored souls remain. Or maybe they're just replaced by the next round of true believers in the Gold Rush dream. In a few years they will join the Middles, obligated by kiddies and jobs, the dream lost in the reality.

17C] Remember WIBBOW.

WIBBOW serves us better than any social media group that wants us to buy their course on selling ads, as if that's the secret in a flooded marketplace. WIBBOW serves us when shysters pitch their services and say they have the answer. Nope. Apply common sense.

Yes, the marketplace is flooded—so we can only have an impact when we have a clutch of books to promote, not when we only have one. Yes, we need to produce more books—on our own schedule. Yes, we will find our way out of the deep dark virgin forest and regain the right track.

What's the secret to success in a flooded marketplace?

- Write interesting stories.

What's the secret to success as a writer struggling with a manuscript?

- Write interesting stories.

What's the secret to success as a writer? Period.

- Write interesting stories.

We need to stop distracting ourselves with newer, better, faster, more expensive. Writing interesting books is the key to everything.

That's our goal.

Then when we track, it's to keep us on track, not to meet a deadline that an outside force tells us is important.

Any distractions—like an online writing course or going to a writers' conference or on a retreat, being with our loved ones to recharge our minds and feed our creative muse—these are not really distractions. They're encouragement.

One simple key. Write interesting stories.

---

[6] The definition of ghostwriter is "the writer whose job is to write the work while someone else receives credit for the authorship" (according to Oxford Dictionaries). Ghostwriters usually work for athletes, politicians, or other celebrities. They will receive "credit" in the acknowledgements, but they will not hold the copyright for the work. It is considered a work-for-hire.

18ᵀᴴ ~ CAREER CHOICES FOR WRITERS

For those just starting in the real world (and school is not the real world. My apologies for destroying that myth), you may be fortunate enough to have a job that offers the hard skills you can use in writing.

Talk to the cranky old fogies. You'll discover soldiers writing military adventures, cops writing police procedurals, nurses writing serial killers, and more. They may fuse genres: military thrillers set in space with serial killers.

Day in and out through decades of work, the skills that these people used on the job are informing the stories that they write.

Even the most soul-sucking, brain-draining jobs can be overcome with will and persistence. Even on the worst days of bloody-fanged work, you can manage a few words, not as much as you want but enough to keep the creative muse and the writing dream alive. The events and skills for those horrid jobs will actually help in writing stories.

I picked high school English as the long-term career. Grading 150 essays by 9th graders every month is not conducive to writing fiction in the evening. Fortunately, I didn't grade those essays every week. When you can find a way to lessen the vampirical workload, grab it.

Like investigative work for police procedurals or the literature / grammar of teaching English, any work will provide hard skills that you can use in building your fiction. Those hard skills, the ones that you didn't encounter in your day job, those you can learn.

Many jobs have specific skills that easily connect to certain genres. Every job offers useable skills for storytellers. Barista skills are more than an ability to calm a caffeine-deprived customer. Customer call centers crack windows into people's private lives. Coaching T-ball teaches you how little children think and what their common behaviors are.

LESSON 18] USE IT ALL

As a writer, everything that ever happens to you, to others, and to the world is all fertilizer for your storytelling.

You can't help yourself spinning "what-if" scenarios. You see something; the creative imp you're training says, "I wonder." Off your brain dances.

That sidewalk café in Old Quebec City. The rocks piled up for a jetty and protecting the lighthouse. The bear cubs prowling around the back porch. That silver-haired retiree in the red dress at the symphony. The hiker, ribbons streaming from his backpack, his photo on the bulletin board at the outdoor store. Even the man who walks his Jack Russell terrier every evening, passing your window at 7:35, no matter the weather.

These snippets feed story seeds and help them sprout. Use everything.

Be smart. Disguise what you take from the lives of close friends. Clever writers convert reality into fiction. Wise ones change specific names and locations, especially to avoid a lawsuit or to avoid offending a portion of their readers.

Real places, real events, real people add verisimilitude to your story. They can also date your story, trapping it in a specific time and place.

These details help readers suspend their disbelief and plunge into the story, forgetting the real world that they're reading to escape.

Reality is your fertilizer. Knowing how to use the details of reality to tell story, that's the writer's first Hard Skill. The other Hard Skills for writing, that's the focus of the next blog.

18A] Soft Skills for Writers

People often focus on the Hard Skills for job success, but it's the Soft Skills that keep people in the jobs that they want.

Most of the early entries are about these Soft Skills for Writers.

Here are the top Soft Skills for the Workplace that also work for Writing.

- Flexibility / adapting to new situations
- Problem-solving / conflict and resolution
- Critical Observation / observing problems and analyzing procedures
- Empathy / being able to understand events from different perspectives
- Resourcefulness / using what's available
- Creative thinking / coming up with new or alternative approaches
- Positivity / approaching each task and day with an expectation of accomplishment
- Teamwork / understanding how characters inter-relate
- Leadership / taking charge of your writing life
- Self-Awareness / analyzing what's working and what's not working

19ᵗʰ ~ Hard Skills for Writers

Hard skills are the teachable skills specific to a particular job.

Lesson 19] What are the hard skills for writing?

Here are just a few. While these skills primarily link to fiction, they also work for nonfiction. After all, factual books make their points with stories about people's lives. Poetry can be narrative in form and is always character-driven. Tilt your head a little sideways, think creatively, and you'll see what I mean.

By the way, these lists are definitely not complete.

19A] Plot

The ability to tell a story beginning to end (plot structure)

The ability to build the center of that story in a way that keeps people interested.

Foreshadowing and Flashback, two tricky terms that trip up new writers. A special kind of foreshadowing is the red herring (also known on Pinterest as "dropping clues").

Sequencing of scenes to create tension.

Building bridges between scenes (sequels. Dwight Swain talks about scenes and sequels in his book *Techniques of the Selling Writer*).

Pacing and Flow. Pacing keeps the story moving like a roller coaster, rather than straight up or straight down. Flow is the coherency of all scenes, how they are tied together.

Suspense.

Theme development and tracking themes through the plot.

19B] Character

Building background and angst

Perspective / viewpoint / point of view and avoidance of head-hopping.

Characterization and character development (two different techniques).

Protagonist vs. Antagonist.

Types of Characters (primary and secondary) / Team Roles / Pack vs. Peck

Motifs and figurative language.

Secrets / Masks / Revelation

19C] Writing

Copyright. The Number 1 thing that every writer must understand. Poor Man's Copyright doesn't exist. If you want to protect yourself, you have to file for copyright. It's not hard; it's just tedious. Don't put it off.

Grammar / Usage / Mechanics. GUM should assist in communicating the story and your ideas. Don't worry about the arcane things. I could list 50 things like consistent verb tense, comma use, avoiding *vial* for *vile*, and more, but I won't.

World Building. Socio-political structures. Topographical structures. Common institutions. Languages.

Rhetorical Devices that create subtle emphasis.

Show, Don't Tell.

Revision / Proofreading. Two separate things. Revision analyzes the presentation of the story. Proofreading looks for typos and grammos.

Writing Marketing Copy (blurbs, ads).

Formatting the Manuscript.

Daily Discipline of writing.

19D] Recommended Masters of Writing

I've mentioned more than a few times Dwight Swain's *Techniques of the Best-Selling Writer*.

Two groups on social media that are extremely helpful are Marie Force's Author Support Network and Mark Dawson's Self-Publishing Formula.

The best writing teachers that I've discovered in recent years for the majority of the Hard Skills that a writer needs—as well as many of the Soft Skills—are Dean Wesley Smith and Kristine Kathryn Rusch.

You can find their classes on Teachable. Look for WMG Publishing. You can also find Smith and Rusch on the internet. They stay up-to-date on information in the publishing and entertainment worlds. Reading, after all, is part of the entertainment business.

Smith has a daily blog covering a wide range of topics. Rusch has a business blog every Thursday. They embody the goal of *Making a Living Writing Interesting Stories.* They are currently hybrid, both traditionally and independently published. They write their own stories; they've done work-for-hire for major publishers. They are prolific because they treat writing as their day job. It *IS* their day job.

As it should be yours.

As of this date, I have no qualms with these recommendations. If that changes, I will update this guidebook. (That's another glory of self-publishing.)

20TH ~ MANUSCRIPT REQUIREMENTS

When I started as a newbie, I understood nothing about layout of a manuscript. *Writer's Digest* helped with that basic nuts and bolts about margins and headers and footers and title pages.

When I started self-publishing, I read through the online distributor's guidebook to determine formatting. I applied that information to my own manuscript, written in MS Word. The formatting guidelines are free and easy to understand.

I don't use any other software apps. MS Word does what I need it to do. I've investigated other writing programs, but steep learning curves and an expense higher than two book covers keeps me from going farther than simple investigation. Some writers swear by Scrivener; others swear by Vellum.

Nothing, however, told me to add in the *7 Common Elements for any Manuscript*.

"Common" simply means that you will find these elements in all published works. Even if you publish independently, you announce your professionalism by including each of these.

A good working procedure is to develop two documents—Front Matter and Back Matter—for any and all of your writing names. Update these documents with every new publication. Then you can easily copy and paste the documents into your current manuscript, already proofed and ready to go.

LESSON 20] 7 COMMON ELEMENTS

20A] You know you need a title. Did you know that you also need a Boilerplate?

The Boilerplate is a unit of writing to be re-used over and over without change. You will find it on the back side of the title page in any printed book. This Boilerplate should also occur on the page following the title in any electronic book. You can model yours on the standard Boilerplate in any traditionally published book.

The Boilerplate is a legal announcement; use it.

A Boilerplate gives copyright information as well as any other publication information, such as the number of the edition of the text. Copyright notification clearly warns unscrupulous persons that they should not reproduce any information in this work without written permission from you.

Place the copyright notification at the top at the boilerplate. If you can't find the circled C copyright symbol, then simply use the word *copyright*.

You may wish to place your writing business email on this page. Marketers, promoters, and licensors who are intrigued by your work will then have your contact information. Fans can also find how to contact you.

20B] Beneath the Boilerplate is the Disclaimer.

All artistic works (novels, films, etc.) have disclaimers: "All characters in this book are fictitious...." Again, you can model a disclaimer from any traditionally published book.

The disclaimer is more legal protection, informing people that you used your imagination and theories to create this work. While your inciting situation might be "ripped from the headlines", the book itself is the work of your brain, not a dry statement of the facts.

Have separate boilerplates for fiction and for nonfiction. Yes, poetry needs a boilerplate, too.

More and more indies are omitting the Boilerplate and the Disclaimer, but I believe that wisdom requires us to follow time-honored business practices that are proven effective in legal situations. Many e-books place this information at the back of the book. Traditional publishers always place it at the beginning. Again, I lean toward standard practice.

20C] Keep a Book List of titles and their series.

Your Book List should come on the right-side page (recto) following the Boilerplate / Disclaimer. (Use a section break to ensure placement.)

This list is blatant author promotion, and it is time-honored. More than one reader has used this list to fill out the missing books that they are collecting by this writer.

Open any traditionally published book by a long-term author, and you will see their books, usually categorized by series or genre and always in the correct sequence (not necessarily the publication sequence). This Book List is an assist to readers, so the chronological *reading* sequence is important.

Like the Boilerplate and the Disclaimer, you can just copy and paste this list into your manuscript, updating as necessary.

On the back pages in many books published by indie writers are the detailed book lists. The books echo the list at the front. This time, however, the point is to hook the reader by teasing them with the book's ideas. Thus, with each title, is the tagline. This thematic hook may be as short as a sentence or may be an abbreviated blurb. "Debutantes should snare fiancés, not murder them" is the tagline for my Regency mystery *The Key to Secrets*.

Writers can also offer a promotional glimpse of the first chapter in the next book. However, distributors like Amazon limit the amount of material in the back of the book to a length of less than 10% of the main text. In 100 pages of story, that means only 10 pages of promotional material.

20D] Acknowledgements and Reader Notes can be at the beginning or at the end.

Most writers and publishers place the Acknowledgement on the right side (recto) before the book's text begins. Simple courtesy is to express your gratitude to those who assisted you with this publication before the publication is read by a stranger.

Anyone can receive your gratitude, including babies in nappies and pets. Many writers take this opportunity to thank anyone who provided research material, editors who helped straighten out problems in the book, proofreaders, cover designers, and family. Some writers add a witticism or quotation significant to the story.

As William Shakespeare said, "So long as men can breathe and eyes can see, / So long lives this, and this gives life to thee." Your dedication gives the person life for as long as this page is available to readers.

Another common practice is to place any *dramatis personae* (cast of characters) before readers begin the story. The "cast list" should be brief. If you have additional information about the characters, your readers are better served by a detailed *dramatis personae* in the Appendix.

Maps are placed prior to the book's beginning.

Reader Notes (also called "Author's Notes" or "Notes to the Reader") follow the book's text, to answer any questions that arose during reading. Appendices are always placed at the end, following any notes.

20E] Table of Contents

In any good word app, you can locate the Table of Contents in the References section of the Ribbon. Really great software allows the TOC to be hyperlinked. Upload your document from that good software, and the online distributor accepts all of your links.

Readers can click the TOC to go anywhere in your book. Writers can, too. I leave my "Navigation" panel (at FIND in the Home section of the Ribbon) open. I can quickly "navigate" anywhere in my document.

I did once think having a TOC was a waste of time. I've been proven wrong. Thanks to all the people who pointed out its helpfulness to readers and writers.

20F] Chapter Headings and Page Breaks

Chapter Headings should never start at the top of your manuscript page. When you wish to start a new chapter, insert a Page Break, hit Enter three or four times, then continue with the next chapter.

Naming your chapters is a personal decision. You will need to mark them in some manner. Chapter number, name of the perspective character, date, location, or a quotation (snippet or entire) may be used.

Mark your chapter headings using Styles in the Home section of the Ribbon. All of your text should be assigned to a particular "type of style", which refers to a common form for the text. *Normal* is for the body text, your paragraphs and the like. *Heading 1, Heading 2,* and *Heading 3* can denote your Main Title, major elements (such as Acknowledgments or Book List), and chapter headings. To assign *normal* and other *heading*s, just click anywhere on the particular line (or paragraph), and the text will conform. To change the heading style, hover over any of the types of headings, and right-click. Select modify to make specific choices as to font and paragraph spacing and more.

When you assign headings, your word processing software will automatically create the TOC. It's genius!

Page Breaks are another matter. You don't want these to show as hyperlinks in the TOC. Devise a method to show the switch of scene or character viewpoint within a chapter.

I sought for several glyphs to serve as my page breaks. Unfortunately, unless I save my document as a pdf, the glyphs turn into gobbledygook when I upload to my online book distributor. I understand that Vellum prevents this and creates a professional-looking manuscript. I'm not yet willing to invest that amount of cash as well as the time needed to learn the program. (Time is the primary factor.)

You can create your own glyphs with symbols available in the word programs that you currently have, my current choice. Avoid any fonts that are not TrueType and any of the unusual symbols. Those two no-no's should help you find something workable so that you do not resort to ## or * * *.

Whichever page breaks you create, be uniform.

20G] A Book of your Book :: What?

A Book of your book is a Master Book. Some people call it the *Bible*. In this you keep all of your background work: character information, plot guides, special information, maps, images, research, etc.

This Master Book will guide you whenever you decide to return to your manuscript. Want to write a sequel? Want to extend this single book into a series? The Master Book should have everything you need.

Much of the information in the Master Book will never make it into your book. That's as it should be. We want to avoid info-dump.

21ST ~ PRACTICALITIES 1

Lesson 20 covered the 7 Common Elements in any book manuscript, whether fiction or nonfiction, prose or poetry. It's easier to say Manuscript Requirements, but then an explanatory paragraph is needed.

MS Prep and Practicalities 1 & 2 is information I've shared over and again since I started my own journey. No one considers these nuts and bolts until starting.

The 7 Common Elements have legal ramifications and offer promotional opportunities. Every manuscript needs them.

Set up a couple of documents that you can copy and paste into each new project, and your Front Matter and Back Matter are easy. Follow the information about the interior Table of Contents, using Styles for chapter headings and having page breaks between chapters. Use subheadings in Styles or set up simple symbolic signals for the breaks on a page.

The most important item in the 7 Common is the Master Book.

LESSON 21] NUTS AND BOLTS OF MANUSCRIPT PREPARATION

21A] Learn the basics for Word Processing.

Whichever word processing program that you are using—MS Word or Google Docs, Open Office Word—learn the basic controls that you will need. Virtually every basic setting can become the default for this and all later documents.

I wouldn't create a template. Default is easier to manipulate if you need to switch things up.

In the *Home* Ribbon, Font is the eye-catcher while Paragraph controls the appearance of the words on the page. If you click the little arrow in the corner of any ribbon box, a pop-up window opens. For Paragraph, click the tab for "Line and Page Breaks" and remove all arrows.

You definitely want to Uncheck "widow/orphan control" and "keep with next". These two UNchecks will prevent big gaps at the bottom of your pages.

Also in *Home* is Editing. Click on "Find", and a Navigation Pane opens to the left. Click in that pane on "Headings", and you can see every Style Heading that you have used. This alone saves you countless minutes searching for information.

In the *Insert* Ribbon, Header and Footer is your friend, for here you will find "Page Numbers". For print-outs, you should always insert a page number, just to keep everything organized. E-books don't require page numbers, so you need to remember to remove them.

Layout is the next important Ribbon to learn. You can change the default margins if you wish. If you are creating a paperback, then "Size" in Page Setup is a great help. Once you have the template sizes from your online distributor (page size, gutter, margins), then you can manipulate your document to echo those requirements.

If you want to create an index with columns, remain in the Page Setup area. You will need to use

Section Breaks before you create the columns.

Finally, in the *View* Ribbon, is an area called Show. If you are inserting images or drawings which will shift around on a page, then select "Gridlines" to help you determine if everything is remaining inside the margins.

21B] **Use the most common fonts**.

When you upload an e-book to an online distributor, you don't want any symbols or glyphs to turn into gobbledygook coding.

You've seen the gobbledygook, I'm certain ~ the ampersand or percentage mark that turns into seven digits of short code. Many more tricksy little symbols abound. You can see them on your screen because they are part of your word processing program. However, when your document converts to an HTML format or the online distributor's coding, the tricksy symbols convert back to short code. If you're not watching for them, you don't see them until you start a read of your own electronic book.

Saving as a pdf will maintain the short code but creates other problems.

You can avoid the whole problem by using the most common fonts. As of this writing, they include the following ~

- Times New Roman
- Arial
- Baskerville
- Courier
- Georgia
- Helvetica
- Comic Sans
- Palatino

Other common fonts are available. You can run a search to discover which ones are current and which have fallen into disfavor. Palatino and Comic Sans, for example, are now considered dated. Some of these common ones, such as Courier, are downright ugly, IMO.

We all have our favorite fonts. While you may prefer a different font, these create no problems across multiple platforms when reading on a narrow or small screen.

21C] **Avoid fancy & charming glyphs and special images**.

Some layout programs, like Vellum, create a lovely document. An example is adorning chapter headings with special glyphs—roses or swords.

While these are beautiful ornaments to the manuscript, your online distributor may charge a little extra for each added image ~ and these glyphs are considered small images. Every image, no matter how small, adds to the size of the file you will upload. Read the manuscript layout information for the online distributor that you use.

A pdf will avoid this additional problem, but other problems occur. The distributor may not want a pdf. The pages may look a little blurred rather than sharp and clear. Again, a little research may save you a lot of angst.

Another element, not considered an image, is the Dropped Cap (where the first letter in the first word of a chapter is much larger). Again, do your research. As of this writing, some distributor programs accept dropped caps; some don't. Other problems with the short coding occurs, with the Dropped Cap not appearing correctly on the page. If you are desperate to use the Dropped Cap, then check for this specifically—every instance—in the online previewer when you are uploading.

For those who truly want special touches, consult a book designer who will understand not only the acceptable types of image files but also how large such files can be--as well as how image files can disrupt the flow of your words.

21D] **Use Page Break for any new section.**

Have a Page Break after the Title Page, after the Boilerplate, after the list of all of your books, and after the Table of Contents and any Acknowledgement. Use a Page Break to reach Chapter 1. A Page Break to reach Chapter 2. And so on.

Otherwise, let the text flow on by itself.

You will have breaks on a page within a chapter. These are not the computer program "page breaks". These are a line of space that shows separation of text. The on-page break represents a shift of character perspective or a change in setting (time, place).

21E] L**et the text flow on by itself**.

Don't use "enter" when you reach the end of a line on your computer screen. Only hit "enter" on the keyboard when you want a new paragraph. Your software will default to have the next paragraph indent itself. Let it.

Consider how you want the page of your book to look. Skim through several e-books and paperbacks. Set up your paragraph formatting for single / double spacing and for "Don't add space between paragraphs of the same type". You will find these selections in the Paragraph box of the Home Ribbon.

I do advise that you check the box that says "Don't add space between paragraphs of the same type". You only have spaces between paragraphs in business documents. Yes, I know your software automatically defaults to this. Your software, however, was developed for business, not for writers in the entertainment industry.

22ND ~ HEREWITH, PRACTICALITIES 2

We have a total of 10 Nuts and Bolts. We touched on the first five in the previous section; now we'll look at the last five.

The section Practicalities 1 specifically addresses manuscript issues.

PRACTICALITIES 2 ADDRESSES PERSONAL PREFERENCES. LESSON 22]

For each of these issues, decide where you will land. Stick with that decision.

You may not think you need to make any of these decisions. Readers, however, will notice if you slide around, following one method or the other willy-nilly.

22A] Oxford Comma or Not?

The Oxford Comma (with the aliases of Serial Comma or Harvard Comma) occurs with items in a series.

> *Pens, pencils, staplers, sticky notes, and paperclips are necessities for every desk.*

The Oxford Comma is the comma immediately before the conjunction *and*. Some people believe that this comma is not necessary. Others believe it is required. Pick which side you land on.

22B] Two spaces after a period or one?

This simple question still causes as much argument as the Oxford comma. Again, pick which way you want, and stick with it.

The use of two spaces does create a larger gap between sentences. When reading on a narrow / small screen, this can look awkward. Most writers have gone to one space between sentences.

However, have you noticed that when you text or email, if you double-space, the period automatically inserts itself? Two spaces may be coming back.

22C] **Print out to proofread your manuscript? Or read from the screen?**

People argue both ways for this. No matter which one that you pick, even if you comb carefully through your manuscript, weeks later you will find errors in the uploaded manuscript.

No one's perfect.

We can get close!

However you choose to proofread your manuscript, here's a statement that every professional agrees with :: While the word processing program has an online Grammar / Spell Check, it's still *not good enough to catch every error*. English is a fluid language (just look at the many meanings of the word "close"). Computers are not fluid thinkers. Not yet, at least.

I personally believe that I find more errors on a print-out than by reading from the screen alone. I do use both methods. Professional proofreaders wash their contracted work through online grammar programs before they spend precious hours reading a contracted manuscript.

Your job is to present the best possible manuscript, whether that is to a pro proofreader or straight to the readers.

If you don't feel up to the proofreading task, hire someone. It will cost money. If you can't hire a pro proofreader, then go to a local source. Whatever you do, don't let a MS out there with "vial" when you mean "vile". It's a huge turn-off to your reader.

22D] Readability Statistics and Passive Sentence Percentages

Here's a nest of arguments.

First, how do you find the statistics?

Go to File > *Options* > Proofing and check the box "Readability Statistics". After you run a grammar / spell check (and yes, I would still do this. The machine does catch problems.), a window will pop up with statistical information. The key items to note are your MS's reading level and the number of passive sentences.

All writers agree that passive sentences are to be avoided. Disagreement comes with how much effort you should spend to remove them.

Basically, try to keep this statistic below 15%. Some will argue that 10% is a better benchmark; however, pushing to remove that extra 5% can sometimes cause twisted sentences that create awkward reading.

- Passive: As they ran uphill, the marathon runners were sprayed by a young boy using a waterhose.
- Active: Using a waterhose, the young boy sprayed the marathon runners as they ran uphill.

The second nest of arguments often arises in critique groups and with wannabee writers, especially the ones who belong to the Ivory Tower world.

Cue a posh accent: *What is the reading level of your manuscript?*

First, the reading level of your manuscript has *nothing* to do with your intelligence.

It has *nothing* to do with your personal reading level (which changes depending on how important the information is to learn).

It has *nothing* to do with your education level.

The only thing that Reading Level has to do with *is* the density of the difficult words in the manuscript. Throw a lot of strange, made-up words that the program's dictionary doesn't recognize, and you can cause the dictionary to stop working. Crowd three-syllable words into long sentences, and you will automatically elevate the Reading Level.

That's not necessarily a good thing. Obfuscation is not the goal; clarity is.

The Flesch Reading Level usually will give an equivalent school grade. Flesch Reading Ease says what it means. Most readers are comfortable at a 7th-to-9th grade reading level. The majority of American newspapers were once geared to a 6th-grade reading level.

Having a Reading Level at 6th to 9th grade is not a bad thing. You want to reach as many people as possible. Don't impress your reader with BIG words; impress them with your IDEAS.

Consider these authors:

- Cormac McCarthy (*No Country for Old Men*) writes at a 5th grade level.
- J.K. Rowling = The first Harry Potter is at 6th grade. The last book in the series is close to 8th grade.
- Stephen King = 6th grade level.
- J.R.R. Tolkien = 6th.
- John Grisham = 6th.
- Tolstoy = 8th.
- Michael Crichton = close to 9th.
- The Affordable Care Act = 12th.
- KJV Bible >> This can cause controversy because several websites list everywhere from 5.8 grade to 12th. That might occur because some books are easier than others. Compare Ecclesiastes to Isaiah.
- Ernest Hemingway's *The Old Man and the Sea* is a wonderfully rich allegory with symbolic dreams and lyrical passages . . . and is written at a 4th grade reading level.

22E] Save your eyes.

This is the MOST IMPORTANT Practical Action you can take. Protect your eyes. They are the windows to your future as a writer.

You are working an arms-length between eyes and screen, right?

Get amber-tinted glasses or turn on "Night Shade" to save the cones and rods in your eyes. Plenty of evidence has emerged that blue-tinted light (especially at night) not only disrupts sleep but causes problems for your eyes' functioning. The amber helps to prevent that blurring which represents damage from over-strain.

Use the magnification in your software. Ramp up the size of the text on screen as far as you need to see without strain.

Finally, take breaks from staring at the screen :: 15 minutes for every 45. If you can't find anything to do during that time, take a walk. Not only your eyes but also your tush will thank you.

23ʳᵈ ~ Eyes on the Biz

Hobbies lead to side jobs lead to small businesses.

People start extras because they love `em or they wanna little extra moohla. As if we didn't have enough to do, what with jobs and commutes and family commitments and social obligations, we get this crazy idea of *More*. We may not see the *More* as a ton of work. Two and three years in, we've got this growing tangle of knotweed[7] that's invading everything and cracking the foundations.

Writers are no different. We like to spin little scenarios. We mull over those until they turn into scenes then chapters. Those gradually grow and grow, taking over spare time, demanding we squeeze in more extra time.

Before we know it, we have a completed manuscript. We bop it back and forth to editors and agents or investigate cover designers and content editors. Traditional route, independent route, doesn't matter. The little darling looks precious, doesn't it?

That's before we realize it's taking over.

And it is nearly impossible to root out.

Actually, we're not even interested in rooting writing out of our lives. We start to think of it as a side job. Once we get a little return, we go, "Yes. I'm in the Writing Biz now!"

So, if we want to call ourselves in the Writing Biz, we need to think like a small business owner.

Lesson 23] We need to write a Business Plan.

The official "business plan" that you'll find after a little searching has five components. (Yes, I know. This no longer sounds interesting. It just turned boooriiiinnnng.)

Business plan models and templates abound. With a little searching, you can find simple and complex, single statements and involved analyses. Whatever you select as your business plan, that plan will soon be radically modified by the needs of your writing business.

23A] Business Plan Sections

- Vision ~ Where do I want to be?
- Mission ~ Why does my biz exist?
- Objectives ~ How will I know when I get there?
- Strategies ~ How do I get there?
- Plan ~ What needs to be done?

That's it. Sounds simple.

Nope.

---

[7] https://www.knoxnews.com/story/news/2019/06/04/japanese-knotweed-invasive-plant-kudzu-vine/1284263001/

23B] Eyes on Your Writing

I wrote my first business plan back in 2016. I backed it up to include my first publishing year, 2015. Early in 2018, I had a lot of split endeavors, things going in opposite directions. I wanted to write fiction AND nonfiction, contemporary AND historical, real AND fantasy. Over the years I have accumulated story ideas for murders and romance, fantasy epics and science fiction. I had vastly different goals for my nonfiction.

Working deeper into the Biz Plan, we should create different objectives for the opposite directions. I tied my different objectives to different pseudonyms.

My original goal was to write everything under my own name. Work-world reality warned against that. I needed a pseudonym.

Research on pseudonyms falls into opposing arguments. Half the people say, "Everything under one name." The other half say, "Nope. A different pseudonym for different types of writing."

I know now that these disparate interests and pseudonyms scattered my focus. A scattered focus isn't smart. I'm in now, though, so I'll keep to the course.

23C] Eyes on Your Expected Audience

Before you launch into your Biz Plan, take a hard look at what you want to accomplish.

If you have split endeavors, seriously consider your audience—because audience will determine success. Part of your success will be writing the best books that you possibly can. Another part will be getting your works in front of the audience in a way that the audience can *see*. A third part is giving the audience more of what they expect.

Pseudonyms fall into audience expectations.

Most readers aren't voracious. They have genres (and even sub-genres) that they constantly read. Cross-over to other genres (and those sub-genres) rarely occurs.

Fantasy and science fiction and paranormal and spiritual all fall under the heading *Speculative Fiction*. In fantasy alone, you have diverse writers like George R. R. Martin and Robin McKinley and Jim Butcher and Holly Black and R.A. Salvatore and Kristine Kathryn Rusch. Most readers don't cross the line from GRRMartin to HBlack. Epic fantasy, urban fantasy, gothic fantasy, grimdark, steampunk, all of these sub-genres and many more, and the readers don't cross-over.

Say you release a steampunk in spring and a contemporary romance in autumn. Both under the same name. Steampunk readers who don't want to read contemporary romance may never come back, thinking that you've betrayed them. It is totally NOT a betrayal, but they won't easily return.

Voracious readers, now—they will read both books if they like your writing style.

So, have different pseudonyms for different genres. I still think this is the better decision. Then you only have to let the voracious readers know you have more writing out there. Create a glass wall between your pseudonyms, and they will step on through, just like Alice.

Understand that you need a business. Your business idea has a focus. You have an expected audience for your business idea.

You're ready to start your Biz Plan.

24TH ~ FOCUS ON THE BIZ PLAN

As we focus on writing as a small business, we must understand our new business' purpose.

First, we determine what we write. Then we look to match our writing needs to audience expectations.

Remember the 5 Components of a Business Plan.

- Vision ~ Where do I want to be?
- Mission ~ Why does my biz exist?
- Objectives ~ How will I know when I get there?
- Strategies ~ How do I get there?
- Plan ~ What needs to be done?

Most small businesses focus on providing one product or one set of related products.

The natural soap maker is making soaps, starting with one and expanding to different scents or purposes. Only after a few years will the soap maker expand into facial scrubs or foot baths. While facial scrubs are *like* soap, they are not *really* soap, but they *are* a natural progression from the original product.

The photographer begins selling framed photographs of general interest: an old barn, a mountain range with autumn colors, a cairn in the middle of a mountain streams, rainbows. Gradually he adds iterations—large canvasses, blank cards, a few calendars. Only after a few years may the photographer branch into true art photography or mixed media.

LESSON 24] UNDERSTAND PRODUCT VS. PROJECT

Writing is not one product, especially when we write in different genres. Each book manuscript is a *project*, not a product. The different forms (paperback, e-book, audiofile) are only different iterations of a project.

What is our product? The genre we write in, that's our product. When we write in different genres, we are writing different *products*.

For each *product*, we will need to have different missions, objectives, strategies, and plans. The only common thing is our Vision. Our projects for our product and the iterations of our projects will fulfill our Vision.

24A] So we ask: Where do I want to be? = Vision

Remember, we're considering our writing genre as our product.

If we want to make money as an influencer, our blogs and podcasts become our product.

If we want to write historical romances set in the English Regency period, that genre is our product. (That's one of mine!)

If we want to write edgy new poetry > or children's stories in rhyme >> these are genres for which we will write the projects that are our product.

If we want to write science fiction romance > or epic alien journeys > or deep-sea explorations with new technologies and working with dolphins > or action-adventure set in the Old West reached through time travel >>> all of these are genres, and the specific genre is our product.

Consider *what* we want and *why* we want it.

Writing a single book—a project—has 12 stages divided into three sections.

Foundation Section	Formation Section	Presentation Section
Idea	Time	Outside Contractors
Genre	Skill	Distribution
Focus	Originality	Marketing
Distinction	Persistence	Next Steps

24B] Our Vision of our production will cover a five-year span. Production = Mission

When we consider our Vision, we begin by understanding the Product we want to present. Then we list the projects that will fulfill that Product.

Since our Mission is Product, we are actually asking > "In five years, where will our product be?"

On the long train of the stages of writing *and* the stages of a project, where will we be with our production?

To complete the Mission = Product, we will have objectives and strategies that will launch Projects from inception to execution.

- We have manuscripts / Projects that belong in the science fiction romance genre.
- The 12 stages take a Project from Idea to Next Step.
- Each Project fits into a Product category, fulfilling the Mission.

The question of *what* we want is the Mission / Product question.

Our mission is to write Steampunk—or whichever genre we want: self-help, yoga exercises manual, fiction, poetry, and so on. When we consider the five-year span of the Vision, we take into consideration the 12 stages of a product, Idea to Next Step.

Now, in this Vision stage, we consider how many projects we can complete in this five-year span.

Every time we add a new Product to the Vision—a different genre, blog writing, et cetera—we expand the Vision. Expanding the Vision of one Product means that our most valuable resource of Time becomes limited overall.

24C] *Why* do you want it?

Now that's the interesting question. The Vision that we want, why do we want it? What is our

Mission to complete?

A Vision placed into a Mission is Dreamed Reality.

The Mission is purpose.

- *Why am I entering the marketplace?*
- *What am I offering that no one else is?*
- *What is deficient in supply that I think I can make available?*
- *What empty hole will my product fill?*

When we consider Mission, we have to be realistic even as we dream. Five years ahead in the Business Plan is far, far away, down the long, winding road. We can see a couple of bends in the road, but not very many. We have to imagine even as we keep reality tucked close to our side.

Don't cripple Vision and Mission. We can do this when we are scattered and unfocused. Yes, we can have different Products. Yes, we can even detour to add in an unexpected Project for a completely different Product. Accept, however, that the panoramic Vision / Mission may try to cover too much. Only a few projects may stand out rather than all of them.

When we have different Products of the same type (all poetry writing, all facial products, all reality-based images / photos), we can have one umbrella business. Different products, though, are different divisions in our corporation.

24D] Therefore, for each product, prepare a Vision and a Mission.

Vision : What will I do? Who will I serve?

Here's a sample Mission statement ~ We help *who* with *what*. Or I write *this* for *market*.

What is the *lack* in the marketplace that we hope to fulfill? This answer considers the five elements that we need to be aware of: demographic, competition, economy, industry trends, and cultural factors.

Here's mine for my Pro Writer series.

Mission ~ To help newbie writers become professionals.

Demographic ~ newbie writers.

Competition ~ Quite a number of professional writers in the indie publishing field are churning out self-help writing books. To stand out, I will need to keep closely focused on my demographic. Titles and marketing copy will have to focus on that element.

Economy ~ Economies of cost are to myself and to my audience. Cost is more than money; time is also a cost. If I make this writing serve double-duty or even triple (a blog series becoming a book), then this Product becomes more economical.

Industry Trends and Cultural Factors can swing drastically over the five-year span. Five years ago, the inclusion of diverse characters in fiction was not the focus that it is today. Diversity is both an industry trend and a cultural factor. For my Pro Writer series, the industry trend is toward more indie writers entering the field while traditional publishing is shrinking. E-books are beginning to sell more than printed books. While the US is my primary market, the Pro Writer series should connect with writers globally.

25TH ~ GUIDEPOSTS TO WATCH FOR

The Biz Plan for Writers can too easily be caught up in an endless stream of project after project. Writers can become so intent on accomplishing goals (those projects) that they lose sight of the original purpose of the Biz. While it can be fun to jump from one project to the next without plan, writers who try to function without a purpose will soon become mired in the muck of everything else in the marketplace.

LESSON 25] SETTING A VISION AND KNOWING THE MISSION KEEPS THE WRITING SHARPLY FOCUSED AS WE MEANDER ALONG OUR LONG, WINDING JOURNEY.

Once we know Vision and Mission, the dreamed reality of our Products, we can start working toward the nuts and bolts of our Biz Plan.

25A] Objectives answer How will I know when I get there?

I can write and write and write—all without focusing on a single work. It's fun! It's also frustrating when nothing ever seems to finish.

Back in 2012, on reviewing my calendars (that's what started my move to a writing business and a Biz Plan, remember), I discovered that I was not writing on a regular basis.[8] No wonder I was a little depressed; my creative muse was stifled by work, work, work.

Midpoint 2013, I knew change was necessary. I created my first, very weak business plan, altered it in mid-November, and tried to push ahead with different versions in December, January, and February. I had no idea what I was doing. I didn't even know I had created a business plan.

A close look at early 2014 reveals six different writing projects, none of them very far along. And no wonder. I was playing at writing. I have other things on this page that have *nothing* to do with writing.

Running a business allows no time to play with our products. We want to have *fun* while running that business even as we generate *some* income.

But ~

Vision and Mission require Objectives to focus our work.

25B] SWOT is you're A-Team

To succeed with any business, one of our first steps in looking at objectives is a SWOT Analysis.

Strengths vs. Weaknesses / Opportunities vs. Threats

When I consider my next five-year business plan, going into it are major weaknesses, the chief of which is Discoverability.

Discoverability is the moment when a writer begins to sell a lot of books. The organization 20Books

---

[8] See Section 5, Thunder and Lightning

to 50K is all about Discoverability. While 20 to 30 is often the quoted number, most people say 30 to 40 is the actual number.

20 is the bridge number, meaning that it starts putting you into the Discoverability range. Newbie status passed at number 7 or so. Pro Writer covers all the writers whose published projects range between 10 and 20, with 20 to 30 as Discoverable. Discovered! is the hoped-for goal, with a steady stream of income.

Strengths are the factors in your favor, the ones that you can control. (Never factor for Luck.) Judge strengths based on ability and expertise, willingness and resources (time, for example). Weaknesses are also in your control. Opportunities are chances that you need to seize (duh!). Threats are also those things that can ruin your career, from outside influences to your own big mouth.

My chief weakness, even after five years, remains Discoverability. As of this writing, I am not close to the Discoverable Range. Under my M.A. Lee pseudonym, I have about nine writing craft books (non-fiction) and fourteen historical mysteries. I shouldn't combine those numbers, and I may even need to split the nonfiction away from the fiction in my distribution—although the nonfiction could drive sales of the fiction. My Remi Black has barely five books and Edie Roones has only three.

Some writers achieve the *Discoverable* range by writing novellas and novelettes. At 15,000 to 35,000 words, these can be produced very quickly, and the industry trends show more writers producing quickly in order to make money. In considering my next Biz Plan, I will add more novellas to my project list.

Continually educating yourself about the writing industry and the writing craft can help you discover your weaknesses, your opportunities, and the threats.

Patty Jansen's *Self-Publishing Unboxed* set teaches an awareness of the marketplace. Having a willingness to learn and try new things is a strength. My biz lacked any market draws, which are hooks to lure in an audience. Market draws are definitely entering the next Biz Plan.

One of the hooks that I need is a repeating primary character for a series. This single element will build audience loyalty. My Remi Black titles (not the novellas) have a single repeating character, but only three of those books are out—Remi Black still has newbie status, not *Discoverable* status. As for my pseudonyms, none of the other books have a primary serial character. In later books a few characters recur in minor roles.

Another Biz Plan change comes from online course from WMG Publishing on licensing. Story elements can be licensed; stories themselves can be copyrighted. For example, the Harry Potter series introduced many elements that had freshness or new-ness. These licensable elements caught people's attention and gave JK Rowling's series a marketplace when they became board games, electronic games, figurines, clothing, and more and more and more.

- Wizard wands are nothing new. Wizard wands containing magical cores are new.
- Unicorns and centaurs and other magical creatures are not new. Hagrid, the half-giant / half-human gamekeeper at Hogwarts is new.
- The train that takes passengers to a magical school is not really new. A train boarded by accessing a station platform "between" other platforms, totally new.
- Harry Potter, the orphaned chosen boy is not a new character. However, the boy with the lightning scar who survived a curse, that becomes new.

- The candies with horrible names and tastes are definitely new.
- The Dementors as soul-sucking haunting evil are not new. Rowling gave the fairy tale monsters new rules and a new focus, and suddenly they sounded new.

25C] Objectives, as any good Biz Plan will tell us, have to be SMART.

- Specific ~ the Product as well as the Projects that will create the Product
- Measurable ~ Results to Measure include sales, profitability (income vs. outgo), marketing, process, and audience. As much as I would like the measured results to be completed projects, they aren't, so I can't count them. The Accomplishments List fits here.
- Achievable ~ Remove any factors beyond our control and work within what we can control. That sounds easy. Very quickly we begin shifting items out of this category. We have realized all of the things that are outside of our control. Project trackers help with this.
- Relevant ~ Projects must match to the Product. Scattering your efforts is not a waste of time but will lengthen the amount of time to achieve your goal.
- Timed ~ Put the Projects on a Calendar and track them. Season to season / month to month / week to week / day to day. Yep, I talked about this in the early sections.

SMART helps us know not only when we have reached our goal (Vision / Mission) but also gives us the path to do so. It aims us toward the practical strategies.

The steps of the Biz Plan are narrowing more and more. We're coming to the Strategies and the specific Plan on this strait, narrow way to your dreamed reality. Next is Getting to Reality.

26TH ~ GETTING TO REALITY

Vision. Mission. Objectives.

It's all well and good to write these three elements of a Biz Plan. Yet in the daily living of that dreamed reality, we discover problems.

Like viewing a new house, all pretty with new paint and clean windows, sunny rays warming the rooms, chocolate cookies on the counter. We think the whole plan is wonderful. We have open public rooms. The kitchen leads straight onto a deck. Enough bedrooms and bathrooms will separate the kids and offer our own private retreat.

- Only when we own the place, only when we're sitting on the couch in the great room, do we stare at the toilet in the hall bathroom. We didn't notice that the bathroom door opens straight into the great room. Not until someone left the door open, and there we were, sitting, staring, cringing. Had the door been scooched down the hall a little, no one would have looked straight into the hall bathroom.

Like anticipating a change at work. We constantly deal with a ticky multi-step procedure that p**ses everyone off. We talk constantly about finding a better way. We even research the problem. Then the boss sends a core group to a day-long workshop—about that ticky yet so necessary procedure. A replacement is in the works. The presenter flies through the presentation on the new software, and the overall process looks easier than the current one. No one gets hands-on practice, but we can see it working.

- Then the software arrives, and it won't work with the accounting and inventory programs. IT manages a work-around that adds steps—but we think the other steps that ticked us off will vanish once the new software takes over. Everything ramps into daily use, and everyone is ticked off even more with the learning curve, the work-around, the hidden steps that the workshop presenter never mentioned. Life is worse than it was.

Or *like the GPS not giving you all the roads* to where you want to go, keeping you on the interstates.

- Only after you arrive do you realize that a secondary road would have avoided the interstates and hours seething at the traffic.

Implementing the new Writing Biz Plan will have its own doors opening into unexpected problems, steep learning curves with work-arounds and hidden steps, and GPS maps that land us in traffic.

LESSON 26] ADAPTATION IS KEY.

As we live with our Vision and Mission and Objectives, we have to adapt them to incoming knowledge. We'll alter objectives, drop one or two, write new ones. We can follow the detours to get where we want to be. Or rip out walls to scooch doorways over a few feet.

Knowing our Vision, Mission, and Objectives will steer us quickly in the right direction. It is the direction we need. Our focus has to be on the projects that create our product, not on writing and re-writing a Biz Plan.

26A] Stay Aware of New Directions [Industry Trends]

In Section 25 I chattered about a new direction for one of my pseudonyms. That new direction didn't just change a single Objective for one pseudonym; it also affected the other objectives and pseudonyms. The overall Mission and Vision changed as well.

Change has to be contemplated, not reacted to. As writers, working with long-term projects, we can't reel from one event to the next. We have to act, not react. To act, we have to deliberate. We can surge forward, but we have to keep our eyes open.

Long-term projects like novels can keep us too busy writing, writing, writing. We focus on reaching the end so we can move to the next project. We use weekly check-off lists, monthly progress meters, yearly reviews and previews, and never reach farther ahead than our current project list.

Awareness *requires* us to step back from the juggernaut writing.

The five-year Biz Plan covers a vast number of days. When we're starting out, getting our business up and running consumes time like a gargantuan monster. Having several manuscripts close to completion was the greatest benefit to my launch.

As I admitted earlier, I wrote my Biz Plan in 2016 yet added in 2015 to include the books that I had already published. I should have backed up to 2013, when I resolved to pursue writing as a small business.

Actually, I should have backed up the Biz Plan to 2012. August 2012[9], just as this is August seven years on. That's when I determined to change.

Hard transitions drive change. Moving across town, away from my old neighborhood and old habits—to a house with a hall bathroom door that wasn't in view of the great room—caused several re-assessments. Writing was only one.

Digging out my old planners, looking back at the previous years, that was quantifiable proof of a disastrous unwritten Biz Plan. I compounded the problem in 2013 and 2014 with another unwritten, unconsidered *Wish List*. It lacked objectives and strategies and a project plan. It did have a mental project list, yet it scattered my focus over several projects. I bounced from one to the next and on to the third and fourth without ever finishing any of them.

26B] Write it Down

This—the single most important point of your Biz Plan :: Write down your dreamed reality, your Vision. Write down how you will accomplish it.

Don't write a *Wish List*. Don't keep the Biz Plan in your head. Write it down. Post it where you can see it daily. Carry it with you. *Live it.*

2012 should be the start date for my Biz Plan, but it will remain 2015. Why?

Because 2013 was as much a wash-out as the previous years. Even though I finished 2012 and started 2013 with a fresh drive for writing, by October I had only 77 days of writing out of 153.

On November 17, 2013, in my writing journal are these words:

---

[9] See Thunder and Lightning, Section 5.

A New Advent of Specificity

"Teach us to number our days" Psalm 90:12

Work to a specific plan.

Focus the Work.

Written goals: long-term, short-term.

I planned to re-set my life. Beginning at that point, I did. In 2014 my planner records writing 33% of the year. I wish I could say that was writing every third day. Instead, the weaker months are balanced against the strong months.

That "New Advent of Specificity" may not have been SMART with a SWOT analysis, but it had Vision, an Objective, Strategies, and a specific Plan.

In 2014 and 2015 I wrote one completely original manuscript, lightly revised two manuscripts to come into line with the new one, and then completely revised an old manuscript that I hadn't touched in a decade.

Writing and revising weren't my only objectives. I needed to decide if I wanted to pursue traditional publishing or independent publishing.

I popped the newest manuscript back and forth to several editors—and received *promising* rejections. How are rejections promising? They say things like, "This is really good but … ."

- But it doesn't fit our current catalog.
- But regency mysteries are not selling in the marketplace.
- But the romance needs to have more heat.

I decided to self-publish. After all, only the cost of a cover would set me back dollar-wise.

Two objectives entered my unwritten Biz Plan:

1] Find out how to create an electronic book to publish. (Among the multiple steps were investigate e-books and e-book distribution, learn how to format an e-book, and create an account with the online distributor > which entailed getting a Tax ID number.

2] Find a cover designer.

I thought 2] would be the easy objective. Nope. 1] was easy. Finding a cover designer with an aesthetic that I liked as well as one who behaves professionally would take 18 months.

In November 2013 I flirted with the idea of self-publishing. It took several, several rejections to turn me off the traditional publishing gatekeepers. June 2014 began my serious search for a cover designer. I didn't find a great one until 2015, and that was sheer happenstance.

26C] Expect Surprises

What you think will be easy won't be.

What you think will be hard won't be.

The writing world will constantly surprise you.

A written Biz Plan that you can adapt will help you tumble with the rolls instead of landing hard and breaking bones.

Next up: Getting to Specifics as we work to the heart of the Biz Plan

27TH ~ GETTING TO SPECIFICS

I've shared photos about my struggles from 2013 to 2016 to turn my mindset about writing from hobby to business.

I count my Biz as starting in 2015, the year that I first published, with four books to an online distributor.

My unwritten Biz Plan started in 2012, and I became serious about writing in 2014. 2015, however, is the Biz start date.

2014	122 days	33.4 %
2015	163 days	44.6 %
2016	259 days	70.9 %
2017	278 days	76.1 %
2018	279 days	76.4 %

Early in my writing journal is this bit of wisdom:
- A goal is a dream with a time limit.
- Set goals. Carry them with you.
- Carry with you what you need to accomplish the goal.

Have Project Goals as well as Mid-Point and Short-Term Benchmarks. These ensure we achieve the Project Goals.

Yesterday and today the key lesson is Specificity, which is not truly a word. A co-worker in my journalism days called himself "Mr. Specificity". He was talking about using the right word, but *specificity* is key to much of life.

Biz Plans require *specificity*. Vision, Mission, Objectives: all have to be clearly stated, clearly quantifiable even as they are the dreamed reality that you want.

LESSON 27] OBJECTIVES ARE TANGIBLES THAT FULFILL THE MISSION.

Each objective is like a fragment of the great stained-glass Vision, your Dreamed Reality.

27A] All areas of your Biz should fit into Objectives.

Fiction Objectives

I have three pseudonyms ~ M.A. Lee for historical mysteries, Edie Roones for medieval fantasies and medieval mysteries (soon), and Remi Black for other fantasies. Each pseudonym will publish works specific to the genres ~ these are the products.

The works are also projects, but a Project List is not an objective. I need to know the reason and audience for each pseudonym. Fill a niche, and find readership.

Discoverability requires that I have about 25 books per pseudo before I can see real growth.

Nonfiction Objectives

I had thought to keep all of my non-fiction under my M.A. Lee name, but fiction readers are usually not interested in writing books, and people seeking writing books merely want to know that the writer is publishing but aren't interested in buying the writer's fiction.

I'm currently considering whether I should split the M.A. Lee nonfiction away from the fiction. I've been thinking about this for a month now. I'll continue thinking about this as I continue to write and publish more books under the M.A. pseudo, both fiction and nonfiction. On the one hand, I have a focused author page on my online distributors; on the other, how will I have any potential cross-over sales from one to the next?

27B] Contract for any Work that you cannot do.

Contract workers in publishing include content editors, proofreaders, cover designers. Funding for all three is necessary. More funding is needed for distribution channels and marketing both immediate and continuing.

The most important contract worker is the cover designer. We have about three seconds to grab a reader's browsing attention: Covers will do that for us. Having a professional eye-catching cover is paramount. Money goes here first.

Many people pay for developmental editing to tell them if they have a worthwhile manuscript and to provide guidance about how to write a finished story. Then they refuse to pay for a great cover. I'm still jaw-dropping about this choice for financial expenditure, and my bemazement hasn't improved in five-plus years.

Content editors focus on the coherence of the story, including plot holes and character discrepancies. I can see paying for a proofreader, especially if you're not that proficient at grammar, usage, and mechanics. Typos and grammos turn off some readers.

27C] Create an online presence for each product (pseudonym in a genre).

Presence means that readers should be able to locate each pseudonym outside of the online distributor channel. This means websites and personalized content for each pseudo's website. It also means creating an email list and issuing updates through a newsletter.

Social media platforms offer ways to interact with readers. These are often the first step taken when a buying reader starts looking for the writer rather than just another book.

A web host provider is essential. A web designer may not be. I paid for a web designer in early 2016. I had expected a steep learning curve. When I took over my website(s) and re-designed them in early 2017, I became much happier. As I learned about the changing website design aesthetics, I did another re-design in the summer of 2018. Keeping the website updated takes time, usually several hours once a season.

Online posts on social media, including Facebook and Twitter and others, also takes time. Posts on your website and most of the other platforms allow you to schedule in advance. Keep an updated log of all of your posts.

Creating personalized content is necessary for all platforms and a newsletter. Readers like to have a connection with an author they've just discovered. Send them too many posts that interfere with their lives, however, and they will remove themselves from any contact with your Presence.

27D] Professional improvement is another key objective.

Writing as a business requires improving skills through reading nonfiction guidebooks like this one as well as attending courses, seminars and conferences. It also requires a constant analysis of the writing process, my own and others, and exploring ways to keep up my interest level for each project.

Online courses are available to help you at all skill levels. These can get pricey. Only pursue them if you have the time and brain to allow the effort that will make the time and monetary expenditures worthwhile. Remember the WIBBOW question ~ Would I be better off writing? ~ whenever you are considered participation.

WIBBOW definitely holds for seminars and conferences. While it can be wonderful to attend these, receiving inspiration along with current information about the genre and publishing worlds, seminars and conferences can be huge time and monetary expenditures. I made Killer Nashville, a mystery writers conference, work also as a writing retreat by attending the panels during the day and writing each evening on my current project.

Taking your writing with you when you discover that downtime at seminars and conferences is making time work for you.

Consider how much information is posted free on the World Wide Web. How much can you find there? Erle Stanley Gardner's story wheels. Victoria Holt's writing discipline. Learning how many previous authors were highly prolific and used glass-wall pseudonyms to "hide" that proliferance.

27E] The Writing Biz requires interaction with other writers.

Writing as a business demands networking with genre-specific groups and general writing groups.

Belonging to a professional organization may not have immediate benefits that you can see. National organizations, however, protect writers in the publishing industry. When a shyster is grabbing for money, the national organizations can send out warnings as well as send the shyster to court for fraud.

Local chapters can give immediate feedback through critique groups as well as give new perspectives on disheartening news. We can learn from each other; we can support each other; we can open doors for each other.

When the groups become poisonous competition, however, it is time to move on. You have a quick answer to WIBBOW when you leave the group feeling badly about yourself and about your writing. I'm not talking critiques of writing here; I'm talking about personal attacks. Critiques of writings should point out flaws as well as provide suggestions for improvement. You don't have to follow the suggestions.

Indeed, Neil Gaiman says, "When people tell you something's wrong or it doesn't work for them, they're almost always right. When they tell you exactly what they think is wrong and how to fix it, they are almost always wrong."

You know where your story is going. You know where you want your career to be going, too.

Here's Gaiman again. "The only advice I can give you (about writing as a career) is what you're telling yourself. Only, maybe you're too scared to listen."

Don't be scared of writing as a business. Keep the day job until you can bank a year's salary along with the job's perks: insurance, pension, etc.. Be willing to pursue the dream in snatches of time until then.

What is your dreamed reality? Vision.

Why is that the reality that you want? How will it fulfill a need for your audience? Mission.

What are the areas that you need to consider as part of your Biz Plan? Objectives.

A to E in this section are the five basic objectives. Your project list is not your objectives.

Objective 1 = Know the Purpose of each Product and the projects that will create them, fiction and nonfiction.

Objective 2 = Know how each Project will enter the Distribution Stream and the funding necessary to get the project into the marketplace.

Objective 3 = Implement various ways to connect with the Marketplace Audience. A worldwide audience demands an online presence.

Objective 4 = Constantly improving your skills will improve your upcoming Projects. Improvement prevents stagnation.

Objective 5 = Have a Network to support yourself and the writing biz.

28TH ~ THE BIZ EQUATION

Objectives can look a lot like Strategies because they focus on the tangibles: what needs to happen.

Objectives, though, aren't Strategies, the scheme, the plotted progress.

LESSON 28] STRATEGIES BREAK OBJECTIVES INTO STAGES.

$$\begin{aligned} &\text{Biz Activity} \\ &+ \text{Expected Results} \\ &\underline{+ \text{How It Will Be Done}} \\ &= \text{Strategy} \end{aligned}$$

Every business needs a product, an audience, and a distinction that will set the product apart from the others in the marketplace. That distinction helps the product find the audience.

As writers, our primary strategy will be to select a book—or series of books—to publish. The stages of the strategy list the steps that must be completed. These steps walk a little closely to the specific plan.

Say your Objective is to start up a nonfiction wing of your writing business.

Nonfiction is a generic term. Be specific. What kind of nonfiction?

Your hobby is photography, and over the years you've discovered enough to enable you to take excellent photographs that sell at local fairs. Each year you answer questions of people who are hobby photographers. They want to know what filter you used or what the lens setting was. They don't understand how to select a better camera than what is available on their smartphone. They can "see" how you selected a certain composition for the photo, but they don't understand the guidelines that you used.

You now have a Vision ~ to help hobby photographers.

Your Mission ~ create guidelines that hobby photographers can easily follow.

From that Vision and Mission you move to a specific Objective ~ Write a book (or series of manuals) that will move beyond basic snapshots to artistic photos. This is the Biz Activity.

You have a specific product for a specific audience. The product has a specific distinction from other similar products in the marketplace.

28A] How will the Biz Activity be done?

Once you list the points that you will discuss—chapters, headings, and points under each heading—you are entering the Strategy stage of the Biz Plan.

Strategies will continue with the following:

- How you will create the product (publication method)?

- How you will pay for the created product (cost of publication)?
- How you will distribute the product (e.g., pricing of product and online retailer)?
- How you will promote the product (ads, fairs, continuing ed classes)?

Some of the areas in the strategy will be long-term. Others will not take very long at all.

28B] In the Biz Equation, what on earth are the Expected Results?

These are the measurements that you will use to determine if your Strategy is successful.

For example, you need to have a projected cost analysis. If you underprice your product, you will not have a sufficient return on your investment of time and money. When you purchase ads, then the cost of promotion has to be added to the cost of publication before you can determine if your product is making money.

Expected Results will also measure the process of getting the product into distribution. Where do you foresee difficulties? How do you anticipate overcoming those difficulties?

Don't forget that you need to tap a finger into marketplace trends, watching for changes in your audience.

As I mentioned earlier, while I was writing a completely new story for my 2015 publication push, I also was researching online e-book distribution and looking for a cover designer. The cover designer was the only true upfront cost that I anticipated in prepping my novel into the marketplace. I didn't anticipate how difficult it would be to find a professional designer with my aesthetic, so the time that I allotted to the search had to be extended.

Had I known about that extended search for a cover designer, under Expected Results I might have changed the deadline date that I had set.

Expected Results will also contain a progress meter or progress list. If many people or areas of a company are working on the distribution of a product, tracking progress becomes vital. For you, with your single strategy of a book for hobby photographers to take artistic photographs, you will have very little that will go to outside contractors. Tracking your personal progress becomes difficult if you have a lot of interruptions.

So, create a progress list of all the steps that you will need, from beginning idea to marketed product.

The first couple of times that you complete this strategy, you will have many changes. More quickly than you realize, however, you will refine your steps to reflect exactly what you do.

. ~ . ~ . ~ .

Writing your Biz Plan should be one of your first strategies in your decision of writing as a business.

Expect your Biz Plan to change drastically, from a single page to multi-page document, from a few objectives to several under each separate product focus.

A Biz Plan is a lot of work and takes a lot of brain power. We need to think about everything we anticipate doing. The Biz Plan saves us uncountable time and energy by giving a clear vision of the Dreamed Reality and the steps to complete it.

And a Biz Plan is not a static document, to be shoved into a drawer and forgotten. As you see and foresee changes, the Biz Plan should reflect your changed direction.

Coming next, we hit the Plan, the day-to-day actions that you will need to take, no matter what you are writing.

29ᵀᴴ ~ PLAN FOR THE BIZ PLAN

We have our Vision, a dreamed reality.

We know our Mission, what will set our Biz apart from others.

We have Objectives for each area of our Biz.

We've set our Strategies for each Objective. We know *how* we will achieve each objective as well as how to *measure* the success or failure of our push toward the objectives.

Now, we dig into the nitty-gritty Projects that create our daily / weekly / monthly / quarterly Plans.

LESSON 29] EACH STRATEGY NEEDS A COUPLE OF PROJECTS PER YEAR.

Work Description (a Project and its Stages)
+ Projected Completion Date
<u>+ Approximate Cost</u>
= Plan

29A] Anticipating Costs: Money and Time

Monetary costs include the Tax ID Number and the cost for the online platform. New writers have the start-up costs of the Biz. All writers will have to hoard up money for any contract workers, such as cover designers.

Time costs cover setting up accounts for other social media platforms and with our selected Distribution Channels. Many social media platforms do not require ads for sharing simple announcement posts. When you create your Biz accounts, get your family and friends to like your page(s). The platforms, though, are cutting down audience "reach", so be prepared if your announcements do not go very far. Use the Time wisely, learning the platforms. When you have a backlist of several novels, that's the time to stretch posts into both the Time and Monetary cost columns.

29B] Plans include four components.

- Projects to complete (books / websites / organizations / etc.).
- Any changes from the previous plan to be implemented.
- Current and subsequent stages for each item on your project list.
- Resources to be developed and implemented.

From my own experience, I will say that I can only work on two projects simultaneously. Having a nonfiction project going during a fiction project allows me to switch out depending on my brain needs. Off days prevent creative work. Those off days include when the night before was a late one or when half the day is errands or appointments or chores. Those days are best for the logic work for a nonfiction project. Creativity for fiction projects requires freshness, energy, dancing ideas.

To work every day on writing, I need the occasional break from pure creativity. Nonfiction projects help me achieve that. If I am not actively writing nonfiction, the off days are Writing Biz days: promos, blog content, bookkeeping, and more.

29C] In the writing biz, we have only three types of projects.

Biz Building—Active Projects :: novels / poems / plays / short stories / etc. This is the list of what I want to write, what I need to write, and what I'm still writing.

Significant Infrastructure—Technology :: laptop plus / website and social media platforms. Marketing :: promotions, free posts, blog content including guest posts, etc. Educational goals :: writing craft workshops, seminars / conferences, online biz blogs to follow, etc.

Ways to Bend the Curve or Trend—Creativity in biz content (making the projects standout), in format of biz content, in marketing, and in distribution.

Five years is far into the future. That's the reason that the second item to include in your Plan are the changes from the previous plan :: what's still to complete, what was delayed, what was gutted / bypassed / yet still a lady in waiting.

29D] Include your WANTS in your Biz Plan.

In 2016, when I considered my "official Biz Plan," I realized that I hadn't attended a true writers' conference for more than a decade, before all the life rolls that changed everything.

The Biz Plan came from attending a one-day seminar hosted by a local writers group in 2015. I had stumbled upon the seminar by chance barely a week before. Most of the seminar's schedule didn't apply to me (the problem with being a long-time Gonnabee), but the Biz Plan was an hour well spent—although I was appalled at the instructor encouraging two college guys to take out a loan to fund their writing biz. Dross with a little bit of gold, as usual for life.

During that session, I roughed out the basic biz plan. I mulled it over for a couple of weeks before assigning it to the back burner.

In a clean-out of my desk in 2016, I discovered the biz plan and decided to finish it out. As part of everything else that I shoved into the plan, I added "Attend a multi-day conference for writers."

Over the next few months, I looked for a conference within a reasonable distance (no airplane for me). The one that I would have attended in 2016 had already passed. In 2017, I uprooted myself from my home stomping grounds and moved 100 miles away (and became immediately happier in multiple ways with my life). I kept investigating writers' conferences. I considered writers retreats. A cash reserve built up, one to use solely for conference attendance, so that everything would be paid for in advance.

Early in 2018 I stumbled upon a post about the conference that I would choose to attend :: Killer Nashville, in late August. It looked to be large enough to have many professionals as well as small enough to be helpful to newbies. The conference also had programming for traditionally published writers *and* indies like me. Several tracks of programming would occur at the same time, offering options.

Killer Nashville fit my needs and my wants. When you look for a conference to attend, take both of those into consideration. I enjoyed the programming, and I used the evenings as a writing retreat.

29E] Also consider the next Biz Plan as you work through the current one.

In looking at my plan for the next five years, I will repeat some things, update others, add what I should have considered but didn't know about, and add the totally new.

One of those new additions will be educational classes.

Another is a constantly updated Accomplishments List, charted by date and pseudonym. When we struggle with the daily writing, the downward spiral into "imposter syndrome" can be defeated by this list.

I have another list right behind the Accomplishments called Wish Fulfillment. I don't look at that list very often. It has projects that had to be shifted to the back-burner on the writing stove. Those projects don't fit my current objectives. I will get to them. That list is important, and I will not trash it.

Here's why. As of this writing, I have published 12 fiction novels under M.A. Lee (with two more to be published this year), four under Remi Black (and two more in the wings), three under Edie Roones (and another simmering for next year), and over ten nonfiction books. And people still, "Are you running out of ideas yet?"

My answer is to think of that Wish Fulfillment list, give them a big smile, and say, "Nope."

29F] Build the Plan

Once you have a draft of your active projects (with each in its formula of Project + Time + Cost, *see above*), you can build a calendar for your plan.

Quarterly first, then monthly and weekly. Keep the daily open for now.

Build in one day-off per week. Build in two days ruined per month. You can always use these days. Life happens. Be prepared. If you don't need the days off, you have four days each month to use or play with.

Also, for new writers, build in two Biz days per month. One day is to work on your budget and the social media posts. The other is to write a personalized blog about your current project. Put your website to use immediately. Not only will you learn the ins and outs, you offer content for readers to have when they search for more information about you after they read your novels.

So :: 4 days off + 2 ruined days + 2 Biz days = 8 days out of 30 every month.

If you are writing every day, approximately 1,100 words per day, at the end of a month, you will have 24,200, which is one-third the length of a novel in any genre. (Fantasy can run longer; romance can run shorter.) And you weren't even pushing. If you didn't lose the 2 ruined days, you have 26,400. If you squeezed in 600 words in addition to your tasks on your Biz days, you have 27,600. If you did the same thing—600 words—on the four days off, you have 30,000 words. None of that required heavy pushing to achieve.

Dean Wesley Smith has a great blog about Pulp Speed and achieving a Million Words in One Year. The old Pulp Writers in the first half of the 20th century regularly wrote that Million each year.

After you consider your months, consider each quarter. Track the minimal that you think you can do, factoring days off.

And consider that for each amount, worked within the scope of each project, for the next four years, aligning your Projects to your Strategies which build on your Objectives to fulfill your Mission that will accomplish your Vision.

The five-year Biz Plan is complete.

Here we are at the end of August and the end of the Biz Plan, and I'm back to chattering about your daily word count.

We have two more sections. Those will take three days.

One more section on the Writing Biz Plan, then it's time for the Hell that Writers Dread and the Heaven that Awaits.

30ᴛʜ ~ Wʀɪᴛɪɴɢ ᴛʜᴇ Bɪᴢ Pʟᴀɴ

It's August, the launch month for my writing business, but I won't write my Biz Plan this month.

I will mull over ideas and collect snippets of info and list potential projects. This in-gathering will run from August into September and on to the last Sunday of November, the first Sunday of Advent.

These months provide the necessary time to contemplate and alter the project list to coincide with the transitioning Biz Plan, old to new.

Lᴇssᴏɴ 30] Aʟʟᴏᴡ ᴛɪᴍᴇ ғᴏʀ ᴛʜᴇ ɪɴ-ɢᴀᴛʜᴇʀɪɴɢ ᴏғ Bɪᴢ ɪᴅᴇᴀs.

For the business to succeed, we have to give it time to percolate the coffee. We can't constantly grind the beans. We can't just brew them over and over. The freeze-dried instant crystals that come through heated plastic don't support success.

We may want to spend all of our time on the exciting project. We also need to give the time needed to support the business.

Remember, the project list doesn't control the Biz Plan. The Biz Plan controls the project list. Any project that doesn't fit Vision, Mission, and Objectives will go to the end of the list.

30A] Review to Preview

During these musing months, I will look back to the very beginning, far before my 2015 Biz start, even before the 2012 Thunder and Lightning Epiphany. I will search for anything that I unconsciously or mistakenly set aside. Should it have gone into my first written Biz Plan? Does it belong in this second one? Should it still wait?

30B] Understand the Failures

I'll also check my Accomplishments List. I'll spend more time checking over my Failures. While we might want to spend time celebrating what went right, we also need to study what went wrong. Disruptions and distractions derail plans. The impish muse enjoys dancing around. Knowing this, I have several questions to ask of each derailed project.

- Why did those projects go wrong? What interfered?
- Did I cause the problem or an outside influence?
- Is it just sitting there, waiting? Does it need to continue to wait, or has its time come?
- Or does it need to shift to the beginning?
- Did the creative muse shove something before it?
- Did I forget about it in the white-hot excitement of a blingie shiny new project?

This series is a great example. I almost didn't start this series. The idea danced in, a classic two-step that wanted to become a waltz. The idea came during the last week of July, but I was trying to focus on my current novel.

- You remember that one. I talked about it earlier. With 10+ chapters still to go, I had reached

56,000 words. The novel was only supposed to be 55,000 words. (By the time I published, that novel achieved 109,000 words). See, I had *better* things to do than a series of posts.

I was three days into August, a sunny Saturday, before sweet little Muse shoved me into a chair on the porch and demanded that I write the 5,000 words she gave me. I needed to focus on *The Hazard of Secrets*.

But ~

Spending Saturday and Sunday on this project gave me time to re-think upcoming ideas for the next chapters in *HoSecrets*.

And this series has now turned into a book, wholly unexpectedly.

The muse will do that to you. She'll zig in what you think is the wrong direction only to give herself and you time to work out problems before you encounter them. At the time, we might blast those new projects as distractions. It's only if we completely pursue the new distraction without ever finishing the original project that we fall into problems.

Throughout August I continue to alternate between this project and the novel project. One kept me fresh for the other.

The *only* reason that I continued to obey that pestering muse was the knowledge that this project *fit* my Objectives and Strategies—and therefore my Vision and Mission. Unexpected though it was, it supported my Biz Plan.

We all have these unexpected additions to our project lists.

As I survey the first five years of my first Biz Plan and look back farther, I will look for the additions that weren't distractions. These should be easily identified. The on-point projects that slowed down word production—those are harder to identify as success rather than failure.

30C] Logistics of the New Biz Plan

The first task will sketch out the new Vision, Mission, and Objectives.

After that comes the Strategies for each objective and the projects that will fit under each strategy.

Last job of all is to determine a Project Plan :: by month, by season, then by year. The creative muse, bless her heart, will need wiggle room in the calendar.

In setting the projects for the past two years, I tried to remove the muse's wiggle room only to have her waltz in with changes. Wiggle room, therefore, is heading back into the project calendar along with room for disruptions and distractions.

If someone offered a six-month RV saga around the Americas, I won't turn down that distraction. After breaking my ribs in May and losing days and sleep to pain, I know that disruptions will occur.

In time for the first Sunday of Advent, I will finalize the overall Biz Plan and next year's work.

- Vision first, that dreamed reality which is achievable.
- Mission second, focusing on what will set my author brands (plural because I have pseudonyms) and series brands apart from everything else in the marketplace.
- Objectives, clearly stated, quantifiable and touchable, aiming toward specific goals.
- Strategies, the steps in the process, long-term and mid- and short-, implementing each

objective.
- Project Plan, tied to each strategy, focused through a calendar—but NOT calendar-driven.

Since we're in the continuing heat of August, Writing Hell is a perfect conclusion for the month.

Writing Heaven, well—that's a harder transition which leads to my favorite time of the year: Autumn.

31ST ~ TRAVELING THRU HELL TO REACH HEAVEN

Dante Alighieri took the circuitous route traveling to Heaven, venturing through a dark wood (*silva obscura*) to the gates of Hell and descending through each level. He encountered whirlwinds and fiery furnaces before traversing the icy abyss and climbing out into *Purgatorio*. He navigated that to reach the spheres of Heaven.

And Dante called his journey *the Divine Comedy*.

Pursuing a writing career is a Divine Comedy. The whirlwinds of constant opinions and constant change can trap us in the early levels, ripping away pages of our manuscripts. The fiery furnace that tempers our writing to improve it can leave us exhausted, unwilling to acquire more burn scars. Then we encounter the icy abyss, frozen out by gatekeepers who block our publishing journey.

When we find a narrow gateway to publishing, we haven't achieved Heaven. The iron-heavy chains of marketing and social media platforms and reviews burden us. Numerous writing sins are extra links that bind us so that we can barely drag ourselves forward.

Yet we can free ourselves of those weighty links and achieve our writing Heaven.

To succeed, we need to visualize our writing *Paradisio*. That vision is all that will draw us through the writing Hell and Purgatory. Will our streets be paved with gold? Do we seek fine mansions of fame? Are we after accolades in our various spheres? Or do we merely want to bask in the glory with constant offerings as our gifts to the great god of writing?

LESSON 31] WRITING HELL

Beginning writing as a career is far beyond writing as a hobby. In writing as a career, you view writing as a daily job that is fun. The daily discipline leads to a completed manuscript, in itself a Hell as we handle character development and plot structures and thematic progressions and personal style and viewpoint tone.

At some point in our writing we fall into the fallacious Hell of Writer's Block. If we misidentify the cause, we may not find the right cure to this psychical disease. The chief cure, however, is the acceptance that Writer's Block doesn't exist.

Whether we're plotting, pantstering, or puzzling, we can easily fall into the fiery Revision furnace.

How hard is it to write the story in our heads?

Extremely. We're distracted by all the things that we think will make the story better. People give suggestions, and the more we have "imposter syndrome", the more we doubt ourselves and listen to them. We can also be entangled by the special little touches that our vanity claims we should add.

I ruined a perfectly good story draft by reworking it to add archaic and obscure language. When I cleared that mess, I discovered character discrepancies. Then my writing style changed—for the better—resulting in another revision. Five versions: *The Tower of Lannoge > Lannoge > Green Wielder, White Sword > Green Wielder > Autumn Spells*.

Only in *Autumn Spells* did I finally achieve the story that was in my head.

It took years for me to learn the Writers 3-Part Mantra:

- Serve the story, not your own ego.
- Write to communicate, not for vanity.
- Know the goal, not the fantasy.

But our Hell isn't over. We dream of our writing being out in the world, which means publishing. The traditional publishing world of editors and agents can freeze a writer in stasis. We can use the time of frozen immobility to learn about storycraft and writing skills—which I did—or we can quit bouncing manuscripts back and forth. We can control our own publication destiny—which I am doing now.

Life Rolls can freeze us for a while, too. Major life changes: marriage, babies, divorce, job changes, job firings, deaths, moves away from home, retirement, down-sizing—these are Life Rolls that can freeze our creative muse as she's halfway through her dance around the project tree.

True writers will come back from the frozen abysses. We find ways around the gatekeepers who can be as vicious as Cerberus. We can recover from the Life Rolls.

We continue writing. We complete manuscripts. We improve ourselves. We dream a new reality.

Once we pass those closely guarded gates out of our hellish Inferno, we're not in Heaven. We have another journey. On our last day we traverse Purgatorio to achieve Paradisio.

32ⁿᵈ ~ Is it Worth It?

We've reached the last section. We mused on our writing Inferno. Now we venture through Purgatory in order to achieve Writing Heaven. Both of these sections are much more general—and metaphorical—than the previous ones.

With this one, we hope to answer the constant unspoken question: Is it worth it?

However, once, you climb down and up out of Writing Hell, your writing life will be much happier. Keep to the commitment. I'm still writing eight years after my commitment to be a published writer of great stories. Most launching writers never make it to five years.

Lesson 32] Writing Purgatory and Writing Heaven take much longer than the newbie writer wants.

Writing Purgatory

We enter Purgatory, the route to Heaven with its attendant trials, with our eyes on our Heavenly goal.

Writing is more than words going onto the page. We have to learn editing, formatting, working with contractors like cover designers, marketing, and much more—all before we release our nurtured baby projects into the wild world.

Then comes the belief that promotions are all we need to achieve our fanciful dreams of Heaven. And shysters emerge, those shills who want to feed on our dream, eating our hope bite by bite. We are burned by bad reviews. The chains imposed by others weight us down.

Yet we have to persevere. Heaven awaits.

No magic can rescue us from Purgatory, only our own hard resolve to overcome any lingering story and writing sins. Money can't bribe our tormentors to free us. Those weighty links will only be lifted away by us.

Only writing will lift those weights. Our writing. Our words, daily accumulating, daily reaching for goals.

What did Neil Gaiman say? "This is how you do it (writing). You sit down at the keyboard and you put one word after another until it's done. It's that easy. And that hard."

And this he said: "You get ideas from daydreaming. You get ideas from being bored. You get ideas all the time. The only difference between writers and other people is that we notice when we're doing it."

And this: "If you're making mistakes, it means you're out there doing something."

As opposed to the Purgatory of doing nothing. And noticing that you're doing nothing. And doing nothing about noticing that you're doing nothing. So that you achieve *nothing*. That's truly Purgatory.

Writing Heaven

What is your writing Heaven? Riches? Fame? Accolades? Best-seller status?

Heaven is achievable. Dante proved it. Once we pass through the Inferno and Purgatorio, Paradisio awaits.

Dante's Heaven isn't like St. John's Revelation Heaven. Your writing heaven will not match other people's. Know that it is achievable, as long as it is a dreamed *reality*.

Keep giving to your writing space with the devotion needed for a 9/5 job. You need not be a 24/7/365. You do need commitment, a vision, and the plan to get there.

I would wish you good luck—but it's not luck.

Serve the story, not your own ego.
Write to communicate, not for vanity.
Know the goal, not the fantasy.

HAPPY WRITING!

INDEX

Accomplishments List ... 11, 30
Acknowledgements ... 20
Amber-tinted glasses .. 22
Audience Expectation ... 23
Author Support Network ... 19
Bending the Curve or Trend ... 29
Biz Building ... 29
Boilerplate ... 20
Book list ... 20
Business Plan ... 23 to 30
Calendar ... 5
Cast of Characters ... 20
Chapter headings ... 20
Character ... 19
Chronological draft ... 8
Competition ... 24
Contract Worker ... 27
Costs, Monetary and Time ... 29
Covey, Stephen ... 1
Creative energies ... 16
Cultural Factors ... 24
Dawson, Mark ... 19
Demographic ... 24
Disclaimer ... 20
Dramatis Personae ... 20
Dream = goal ... 1
Dream vs. fantasy ... 3, 7

Dropped Cap ... 21
Economy ... 24
Ellington, Duke ... 1, 3
Expected Results ... 28
Failures ... 30
Flesch Reading Ease ... 22
Font selection ... 21
Force, Marie ... 19
Formation ... 24
Foundation ... 8, 9, 24
Gaiman, Neil ... 27, 32
Global draft ... 8
Glyphs ... 21
Grammar / Spell Check ... 22
Guardian ... 7
Hard skills ... 16, 19
Harry Potter ... 12, 25
Heaven ... 32
Hell ... 31
Homer ... 12
Iliad ... 12
Images in manuscript ... 21
Imposter syndrome ... 11, 14
Industry Trend ... 24
Inertia ... 14
Infrastructure ... 29
Innovation ... 13
Invention ... 13
Jansen, Patty ... 25
Killer Nashville ... 9, 10
Licensing ... 25
Linear draft ... 8
Mantra for Writers ... 1, 32
Maps ... 20
Master Book ... 20
Mission ... 23 to 30
Modeling ... 12
Networking ... 27
Objectives ... 23 to 30
Online Presence ... 27
Over-planning ... 9, 11
Oxford Comma ... 22
Page breaks ... 20
Pantster ... 8, 13
Passive Sentence ... 22
Plan ... 23 to 30
Plot ... 19
Plotter ... 8, 13
Presentation ... 24
Procrastination ... 14
Product ... 24
Professional Improvement ... 27
Progress checks ... 6, 10, 11, 14

Project ... 24, 27, 29
Pseudonyms ... 23
Pulp Fiction ... 12
Purgatory ... 32
Puzzler ... 8, 13
Ramsey, Dave ... 4
Readability Statistics ... 22
Reader's Notes ... 20
Reading Level ... 22
Refusal ... 14
Rowling, J.K. ... 12, 25
Rusch, Kristine Kathryn ... 19
Scattered draft ... 8
Self-Publishing Formula ... 19
Self-Publishing Unboxed ... 25
Shysters ... 17
SMART ... 25
Smith, Dean Wesley ... 9, 19, 29
Soft skills ... 18
Space for writing ... 6, 7
Strategies ... 23 to 30
Styles ... 20
Swain, Dwight ... 14, 19
SWOT ... 25
Table of Contents ... 20
Tarantino, Quenton ... 12
Text flow ... 21
Toxicity ... 17
Vision ... 23 to 30
WIBBOW ... 4, 16, 17, 27
Wish Fulfillment ... 29, 30
Word counts ... 6, 10, 11, 14, 29
Word processing ... 21
Writer's block ... 14
Writers' Rooms ... 7
Writing skills ... 19
Writing space ... 6, 7

Blatant Self-Promotion

In the nonfiction guidebook by M.A. Lee, *Discovering Your Novel,* are various writing techniques After fitting together the story bones to make its skeleton, we fill in with the flesh, organs, muscles, and other tissues.

Discovering Your Novel is designed to help a newbie writer complete a book in one year. 365 days of guidance for your writing. With Charts! ;) After 25 novels, my process is much more stream-lined than this one, with much of it internalized, yet *DiscNovel* truly presents a workable model for any writer.

If you have a manuscript that you think is lost to you, it's not. You can also use *Discovering Your Novel* to diagnose the problems with the manuscript. Repair the damage, take it off life support, give it the necessary healing, and then send it into the world.

#BSP #2.

If you're looking for a way to build the daily discipline of writing, you can set up your own word count tracker and project progress meters.

If you're not into that, then M.A. Lee has a planner as well as several charts that can help you. You can find the planner here. The Think/Pro Planner for writers has a place to track daily word counts, weekly progress meters, monthly reviews and previews as well as seasonal project planning and yearly reality checks.

If you just want charts to help you build a writing discipline, then visit the Writers Ink nonfiction website. This link will take you to the Pro Writer Advice page with free charts from my writing craft books. Check out the charts from *Discovering Your Novel*.

Finally, #BSP 3.

If you want to know more about developing characters and plots, these two writing books give guidance.

Discovering Characters offers everything you need to know about—well, characters. From individuals to teams, pecks and packs, along with all sorts of classifications, the manual is a great reference for your writing shelf.

Discovering Your Plot will cover the 7 types of plots as well as the five major plot structures, with detailed guidance for the archetypal story pattern. Classic tropes (*pet the dog*) can help you imagine scenes, but they don't help construct novels. *DiscPlot* gives clear examples from well-known works of literature.

For charts and print-outs, check the Pro Writer Advice page for Writers Ink.

There, #BSP over.

THANK YOU!

Thank you for reading *Inspiration 4 Writers*. Did you find a few doors to unlock to open passages to your writing career future? That's always the hope.

When Edie Roones and M.A. Lee made the leap into indie publishing in 2015, we made several mistakes. Indie publishing was still relatively new and not a lot of information was available for the self-publishing marketplace. Truly, the daily life of the writer is still not widely available in any marketplace, whether self-published or traditionally published. This *Inspiration 4 Writers* series is intended to help other new writers avoid the early mistakes.

For any questions, comments, and speculations, please contact winkbooks@aol.com. All Writers Ink titles can be about on the website along with purchase links ~~ www.writersinkbooks.com

Writers Ink doesn't collect email addresses or use affiliate links. Nor will we bombard you with newsletters or the like. We've got writing to do. W.Ink doesn't use ghostwriters or work-for-hire writers or collaborators. Beta Readers and proofreaders, however, are always helpful. If you spot an error, please let us know. As soon as possible, we will correct the errors and re-upload, which will make available to you an updated novel file.

Indie writers thrive on reviews. With *any* book that you enjoy, please share with other readers looking for escape from the stresses of life.

DREAM IT. BELIEVE IT. DO IT.
~~ *M. A. LEE, REMI BLACK, AND EDIE ROONES*

HEARTS IN HAZARD BY M.A. LEE

Mysteries with a dash of romance, set during the Regency Era of England:

1 ~ *A Game of Secrets* ~ Smugglers, secrets and spies: Kate tries to hide in plain sight; Tony tries to catch a spy. First they fall in love; then they fall into trouble with smugglers. Will they survive?

2 ~ *A Game of Spies* ~ Salons and soirées, flirtation and dancing, gambling and spies: Josette and Giles fall in love over a deck of cards and try not to die. Spymaster Giles Hargreaves was introduced in *A Game of Secrets*.

3 ~ *A Game of Hearts* ~ Two couples :: One titled widow, one wealthy businessman: two hearts shadowed by their past. One bright young flirt, one hard-edged young man: two hearts crossed by circumstance. Mix in a courtesan and two rakes, all out for mischief, and murder bloody and foul.

4 ~ *The Danger of Secrets* ~ Deep in the wintry countryside, a house warmed by relatives and friends: secrets of family, secrets of hearts, secrets of blood and pain. Match a daughter to an unknown father; match a spinster to an earl; match a serial killer to his next victim. (Gordon Musgrove was introduced in *A Game of Spies*.)

5 ~ *The Danger for Spies* ~ Impossible: rakes don't lose their hearts. Impossible: spies don't give up the game. Impossible: no one hides in plain sight. Impossible: codes are unbreakable. Impossible: a man can't hold onto revenge for years and years. Impossibilities are designed to be shattered. (Toby Kennitt was introduced in *A Game of Spies*.)

6 ~ *The Danger to Hearts* ~ A country manor in early Spring: older woman and younger man. Horses, cats, needlework, roses and afternoon teas ~ what could possibly go wrong in an idyll? Trouble in the past, trouble now, and murder. (The character Joss Carter was introduced in *A Game of Secrets*.)

7 ~ *The Key to Secrets* ~ Debutantes should snare fiancés, not murder them. Constable Hector Evans (from *The Danger to Hearts*) returns to solve three murders. Is his former love guilty of murder or a convenient scapegoat?

8 ~ *The Key for Spies* ~ Spies and traitors. Lies and treachery. Unexpected love where bullets fly. One traitor destroys loyalty. What will two traitors destroy?

9 ~ *The Key for Hearts* ~ A convenient marriage inconveniently causes murder.

10 ~ *The Hazard of Secrets* ~ Two hearts with dangerous pasts—Can they keep their secrets, or will murder force them to reveal all?

11 ~ *The Hazard for Spies* ~ Disguised spies, disguised motives. When the marks are removed, will the truth be revealed? Or will the murderer find them?

12 ~ *The Hazard for Hearts* ~ Two wives haunt the castle. Will she become the third wife to die?

INTO DEATH SERIES BY M.A. LEE

Digging into Death ~ A governess seeking refuge, a handsome young man, an archaeological dig: romance is inevitable; murder is not. Suspicions escalate, artifacts are stolen, and then a second murder. Has the love of her life beguiled her straight into death? Available in paperback and e-book

Christmas with Death ~ Christmas is for miracles, merriment, and murder. Set in 1919 at an English country manor for a party throughout Christmastide. Available in paperback and e-book.

Portrait with Death ~ coming soon

NONFICTION BY M.A. LEE

Think like a Pro Writer series

Old Geeky Greeks: Write Stories with Ancient Techniques

Think like a Pro: New Advent for Writers ~ available in paperback and e-book

Think / Pro: A Planner for Writers An undated planner with daily word counts, progress meters, project planning, and goals analysis. Paperback only. How else will you record your goals and progress? Two different covers available.

Discovering Your Novel ~ a 52-week course for new writers, offering guidance from idea to publication and marketing.

Discovering Characters ~ Delving deeply into your primary characters entails more than just template and character interviews. You also need to know your secondary characters. You need to present more than appearance, more than intellect; your characters have a heart and soul. Discover them!

Discovering Your Plot ~ The varieties of plot that structure all novels, and M.A. Lee's choice for the best working plot structure for writers.

Discovering your Author Brand ~ Revealing the secrets that catch reader's attention as you brand your book, your series, and yourself as the author. With examples and explanations from past successful marketing efforts.

Discovering Sentence Craft ~ Zeug-what? Chiasmus? Auxesis? Are any of those spelled correctly? Well, yes. These are literary devices used for centuries by the best writers to make their works memorable. Writers are artists, seeking ideas from the creative muse. We're also crafters, looking for the best ways to present those creative ideas. DiscSCraft presents techniques for using figurative & interpretive concepts as well as the structures of inversions, repetitions, oppositions, and sequencings.

Inspiration for Newbies ~ *Just Start Writing* (this book)

2 * 0 * 4 Lifestyle series

2 * 0 * 4 Lifestyle: Transform Your Whole Self (coming soon)

2 * 0 * 4 Lifestyle: A Planner for Living Using Luke 10:27 for the whole self—heart, soul, mind & body—an undated planner to help you muse and move, feast and fast, and live and love. Paperback only. How else will you write in it? Seven covers available: Meadow (my favorite), Floral, Woodland (for hikers), Mountain River (my second favorite), Cityscape (with the Henley Street Bridge in Knoxville as the focus), Teatime (in the garden), and English Cottage (with spiced tea on the back cover).

Remi Black, fantasy

Fae Mark'd Wizard

Wizard against sorcerer. Fae against dragon. Wyre against Rhoghieri.

Weave a Wizardry Web

Least becomes great. Greatest becomes least. Two wizards travel sharp-bladed roads in *Weave a Wizardry Web*. When a wyre pack begins hunting one wizard, and the other practices a sharing linkage one time too many, will they survive the sharp blades on their chosen roads?

Dream a Deadly Dream

Assassination. A fugitive comtesse. A lethal sleep-spell. Wyre and wraiths. Wizardry against sorcery. And regicide. In *Dream a Deadly Dream*, a sorcerous plot to kill the king weaves together past and present, dream and reality, to create a nightmare that can kill.

Sing a Graveyard Song

Can Alstera defeat Death Walking before it takes yet another life? Will the Enclave tracker decide that she must have her powers stripped completely away? Or will wielding blood-magic against a blood-spelled creature force Alstera across the tenuous barrier that separates wizardry from foul sorcery?

Wield a Fae-Sharpened Sword (coming soon)

Kindle a Dragon's Fire (in the sketching stage)

Dance to Bone-Edged Music (in the sketching stage)

Fae Mark'd World: Spells of Air

To Wield the Wind: Enclave World 1 ~ published Spring 2019

On a mission for the Wizard Enclave, Orielle ventures into the Wilding, a strange frontier filled with magical creatures. There she discovers sprites and wraiths, gobbers and wyre. All view her as prey.

To Charm the Wind: Enclave World 2 (coming soon)

To Curse the Wyre: Enclave World 3 (sketching stage)

Edie Roones, fantasy

The Seasons in Sansward Quarternary

Summer Sieges

Honor and death? Or cowardice and life? Stark choices, and not that easy. Can Beren survive a journey through the Shadow Path and battle with the Watrani? Or will she sacrifice herself in another futile attempt to guard the Eye?

Autumn Spells

Can the Green mage Saisha free the swordsman Hethan from a dark dame's foul sorcery? Or will Neehla's dark spells trap them both?

Winter Sorcery

When a Gitane WitchMaster pursues two Frenc spies who stole a sphere of power, can a half-trained mage and a simple temple cleric help them escape?

Spring Magicks

(in the sketching stage)

All books from Writers' Ink are available at Amazon.

For any comments, questions, and speculations, contact winkbooks@aol.com. Use the subject line to direct your email to a specific book or series.

www.ingramcontent.com/pod-product-compliance
Lightning Source LLC
Chambersburg PA
CBHW080436110426
42743CB00016B/3179